Reflection of Christ

God's Power Inside the Prison Cell

Martin Tuson

authorHOUSE™

1663 LIBERTY DRIVE, SUITE 200
BLOOMINGTON, INDIANA 47403
(800) 839-8640
WWW.AUTHORHOUSE.COM

First published by AuthorHouse   2/17/2006

ISBN: 1-4259-0816-0 (sc)

Printed in the United States of America
Bloomington, Indiana

This book is printed on acid-free paper.

Dedication

I dedicate this book to my wife Margaret and my two beautiful daughters Hannah and Laura.

You may ask yourself - "why prison?" Why should God's love be demonstrated amongst people who cause others pain? I can only reply to that by saying, "It is the sick that need a physician, not the righteous." Maybe by God demonstrating His power and love inside these prison walls is a witness to us sinners of the love that we need to give back.

Table of Contents

Foreword

It is a privilege and a pleasure to write the foreword to this long awaited book by my friend Martin Tuson. I have known Martin for fifteen years and have watched with awe the development of his ministry within the prisons here in Northern Ireland and worldwide via correspondence. Martin is a dedicated, humble and committed man who has seen first hand the miraculous power of God at work in what would be considered some of the most dark and ungodly places in our land.

As a family man with a lovely wife Margaret and a beautiful wee daughter Hannah, Martin never ceases to amaze me with his love and commitment to those men and women who are in prison. He, and I'm sure he wouldn't mind me saying, is not the most likely person to be seen 'walking the wings' of the prison system, but his love for these prisoners is infectious. Where 'angles fear to tread' Martin doesn't.

This book will inspire you to see what God can do when we trust Him. The miraculous power of healing and deliverance, the true life stories of men seeing God work in dynamic ways, the world wide Ministry through correspondence and the prayers that know no bounds, setting people free from the 'prison of sin', bringing hope in despair, peace in the midst of turmoil, all will leave you breathless and make you praise and thank God. You will laugh and cry from the humour of the 'budgie' story to the life changing stories of men whom society has given up on. In it all, you will see how great our God is, how He can take a quiet, faithful servant and use him in such a powerful way.

It is my earnest prayer that you read this book and let it affect your life.

Luke 4:18

Pastor David Beckett
Bangor Elim Church

Introduction

Psalm 105. 1-2 " Give thanks to the lord, call on his name; make known among the nations what he has done. Sing to him, sing praise to him; tell of all his wonderful acts."

Through this book you will come to know and see the *Wondrous Grace, Mercy, Love* and *Forgiveness* that Christ has for those who are afflicted and needy within the darkness of the prison cell. My prayer is that as you read through the following chapters, you will be encouraged in your faith. For those who do not know Christ as their own Lord and personal Saviour, I pray that you will come to accept him and know that He is indeed very real.

For those who have fallen away from Christ, I pray that the joy of your salvation will return, for those who are suffering through sickness, my prayer is that you will be healed and that your faith will rise when you read of Gods healing power through these pages.

When you pick up the paper or switch on the News or listen to the radio, you will always hear prison being spoken of in a bad light. Sadly there are not too many reports on the good things that take place within the prison cell.

God is moving as never before amongst inmates throughout the world.

I thank God for the opportunity to write this book. Every word you read is true and really happened. You will see how God can take an individual like myself and call me to such a powerful Ministry.

Each one of us has a call on our lives and God is looking for an obedient heart.

I used to sit in church and think to myself, "What can I do for God?". Let this book be an encouragement to you.

I give my precious Lord and Saviour Jesus Christ all of the Glory and honour that is so rightly due to His name.

For all that is written in the following pages of this book is a powerful testimony to the Saving Grace of Christ.

Martin Tuson

Chapter One

~ A Call to Serve ~

"That's very good. Who wrote that?" This was my wife Margaret's reply to me after I had showed her the first poem that I had ever written. Little did I know back then that this was God preparing me for the years, which lay ahead.

It was in my work place that many of the poems I wrote took place. Yes, God inspired me to write such poetry. There was indeed a plan for each one of these poems. Back then I wrote, as I was lead by God's Spirit. The poetry consisted of God's love towards the broken hearted and oppressed.

It was then in 1996 my Christian life started to take on a new meaning.

As a young and frightened boy of 15 years old, I gave my life into the hands of the Master. On the 7th November 1982 I received Christ as my Lord and personal Saviour. That glorious day I was born into Gods Kingdom. I could scarcely have imagined back then the things I would witness 20 years on.

The poetry for many years gathered dust on a shelf in my cupboard. The odd time I would pass one or two onto some people within my local church. Then at the end of 1999, God directed and led me to have sixteen of these poems placed into a booklet. In June 2000 "The Only Way" was published. Two hundred copies were printed and I decided to raise some money for a Christian Ministry through the sale of the booklets.

Then in June 2000, the last Friday of the month, I was to have an encounter with the Lord Jesus himself. That night my life was changed forever as the Lord opened my eyes to what lay ahead for me. On that night my wife and wee daughter Hannah had retired to bed. I sat downstairs in the living room watching T.V. I was not thinking about God at this time. It was about 10.00 p.m. and as I sat on the sofa, I experienced something which had never taken place in my Christian life before. God spoke to me. Yes, I know many may think - what do you mean He spoke to you? This was no audible voice, but it might as well have been for all of a sudden within my head and most of all in my heart He spoke. He said *"Martin, I want you to send your poetry into the prison system".* That was it, within a few seconds my heart rate went through the roof, I was out of breath and I had not even moved. I can't fully describe the feelings that came over me then. The seed had been planted. Immediately I ran upstairs. My heart was bursting. I had to tell someone. I woke Margaret from her sleep. I told her that God had spoken to me about prison. I think I shocked her slightly as she was not used to being woken up suddenly. She told me that we would talk more in the morning.

My heart was still racing. I wanted to shout it from the roof tops.

I walked back down to the living room and as I entered my eyes fixed on the T.V. there in front of my eyes there was a man standing in a prison sharing the love of Christ with the inmates. God's small still voice spoke once more to me. **"Martin I am going to take you and use you within the darkness of the prison cell".** I wept like a child that night.

The next day I arose and was a different person than the previous day. For I woke with a calling on my life to reach out to the inmates with the Grace, mercy, love and wonderful forgiveness of Christ. The journey was about to begin and little did I know back then, that in the years, which lay ahead, I would witness the power of God in such a wonderful and awesome way. I tell many people that the only way I can describe what took place that night is as if I was lying on an operating table and Christ was the heart surgeon standing over me. He opened up my chest and my heart lay bare. He then took a small package and on the side of this he took a thick black marker and wrote the word "INMATE". He attached this package on to my heart and sewed me up again. When my heart beats I feel this package within, for Christ gave me His eyes with which to see these people.

You know, many people will stop and talk with me and many will talk of incidents that have taken place in their past, to do with crime etc. They say to me that they will never be able to forgive certain folk for what they have done to them and to others.

My reply is, "No", you can't forgive them, the only way you can forgive them is if God first does his work in your own heart and gives you the Grace to forgive. For today I am involved with many people who have committed terrible crimes, yet despite this I love them through Christ.

It is only through Christ and His Grace that I am involved in this Ministry to the incarcerated.

You know when God touches you and gives you his precious Grace, you can do things that you would normally run from.

Just after that powerful night on which God spoke to me, he started to open many doors. The poetry books were sent into many of the prisons within the British Isles. Chaplains started to write and ask me to send more. God used that little booklet in a mighty and powerful way. In the beginning the booklet was sent to thirty prisons. Many of the names you will be familiar with Wandsworth, Brixton, Parkhurst etc. The following is a reply from one of the chaplains: -

HMP SEND   24th October 2000
Ripley road
Send
Woking   From the prison Chaplain
      Reverend Andrew J. Foran
Martin Tuson   St. Barnabas Chaplain,
      HMP Send

Dear Martin,

Thank you so much for writing to me and enclosing a collection of your poems, "The Only Way"

I have read some of the poetry and you are clearly inspired by the Lord to write such touching and deep, meaningful, life-engaged words. I know that our women in this establishment will greatly benefit from your writings as they engage and express very noticeably with matters of emotions and Spirit.

I would like therefore to take up your offer and ask you to send me 20 copies at your convenience. Please advise me of the cost.

Please send to me at my above address.

Every blessing in your Ministry,
Yours sincerely,
Andrew J. Foran

In total 1400 more booklets were sent to the prisons in the British Isles. You may wonder how I managed to be able to have all of these printed. Well this is where the story of God's provision started. For even then with my weak faith, I decided to trust in God and not in man. I made a decision from that night. I would never stretch my hand out to man for anything.

Chapter Two

~ God's Provision ~

Only a few weeks after the Lord spoke to me about Prison Ministry, he told me to send 600 copies of "The Only Way" into thirty prisons. He gave me the names of these prisons in a mighty way. (That's another long story). I was well aware that this was going to take a large amount of finance. At this point I would like to say that you would usually never hear me speak about money, but it is important to let you know about God's wonderful provision and that when you trust in Him, He will meet your every need.

The very day the Lord told me about this, Margaret, Hannah, and myself went on a family day trip to Newcastle. On the way there in the car my mind was doing overtime and even with my great faith I thought of some sort of sponsored event (Either a cycle or run). God spoke to me through Margaret and reminded me that it was He who would meet that need. So for the rest of this day my mind continued to think about this need. That night we arrived back home just as my mum called. God's timing is perfect. Margaret went into the kitchen and started to make a cup of tea. It was then that my mother handed me an envelope, she said that her friend's son gave her this to give to me. On the outside of this envelope it said "Poems for Prison". I opened it and Praise God it was the full amount that I needed to send out the books. The hairs on the back of my neck stood up that night. Margaret and my mother also were in awe of God's Provision.

From that day nearly four years ago to the time of writing this, God has met our every need. I could write a book itself on the Lord's supernatural provision for this Ministry. So many powerful miracles! Again He has been faithful to me and I am so thankful. At times it can be very difficult and my faith is stretched but I can always testify to God's gracious goodness. For it's only through Him that we have been able to send thousands of pieces of literature into many prisons throughout the world. I started to be in contact with other prison Ministries. One of these Ministries, which was called Matthew 25, is a powerful Ministry run from Johannesburg, South Africa. Through this Ministry the poetry books were sent into Max Security Prison Zambia a prison that I was going to be heavily involved with in years to come. The books also made their way over to the U.S.A. At this stage the Lord started to speak to me about a magazine solely for inmates. This magazine was to be a miracle in the making.

One night, whilst in work, the Lord gave me the idea of this magazine. He gave me the layout and the title. It was to be called "SET FREE" a very appropriate name for a prisoner's magazine. The Lord gave me the whole first issue that night. It was to consist of eight pages, nothing fancy. Issue one was printed in 2001. One thousand copies were produced, and again sent into prisons with which we were involved. Again the Lord was working and this magazine was laid out in such a way that those who struggled with reading would be able to read it more easily. The print was big and mainly contained poetry and scripture with some articles I had written. One poem, which was written in this first issue, was called "No Words". I would like to share this with you for it speaks personally about my own thoughts.

"There are no words for me to say,
to show how grateful I am today,
for your great love on Calvary,
which broke this heart and set me free.
Dirty rags now are clean,
Since my saviour's face I've seen.
A graceful God who gave his best
In him I trust my soul does rest".

At this stage of the amazing journey many new doors were being opened by the Lord. The night that Christ met with me in June 2000, he spoke to me and told me that he would use me within the prison cell. I knew that one day he would physically take me and use me in this way. "But Lord, I thought, how do you even begin to enter a local prison in Northern Ireland?" Only a few weeks later I was standing in HMP Magilligan taking two meetings. Nine months to the day God called me, I was reaching out to inmates. What another powerful miracle! Again words fail me. The Lord was to draw me ever closer to Himself and my calling to those afflicted and needy men and women within the prison cell.

Chapter Three

~ A Night to Remember ~

On the Thursday night I headed up to Magilligan. After a quick stop in Coleraine for a bite to eat, I proceeded to the prison and arrived in good time.

The first meeting took place in the main section of the prison, in a portacabin off the main wings. There was a keyboard there and it looked as if there might be singing. Many people asked if I was frightened entering into the prison that night. I can honestly say from that day to now that I have never experienced fear within the prison walls. More excitement than fear! I know that my God is with me, protecting me. He goes in front and behind. The inmates started to arrive. All together about 15 or so came to the meeting. What a powerful time of worship! I will never forget the singing. Remember, most of these guys did not have the Lord in their life. It came my time to speak. I had hardly ever spoken before at any meetings and here I was about to address 15 inmates. Praise God for the power of the Holy Spirit, which enables us to witness for him.

I remember well that night that a bit of a debate started regarding God's supernatural power to heal. One of the young guys at the front interrupted me, when he saw me lift up my poetry book. He said that he remembered this when he was in the young offender's centre. He remembered the cross on the front cover. This young man could neither read nor write, yet the cross spoke to him. I will never forget that young man. After the first meeting the guys shook my hand and thanked me for coming to speak to them. It was a wonderful opportunity to hand them a copy of the "SET FREE" magazine.

The second meeting was in the working out area, were inmates are close to their release dates. It was at this meeting that I felt I wanted to spend time individually with each of the guys. There were 5 or 6 inmates there and again it was a wonderful time in God's presence. One of the inmates spoke to me and told me that no one from his church had bothered to come and see him, including his Minister. It gave me a perfect opportunity to speak to him. I told him that unfortunately, in life people, including friends and family, will let you down. I then went on to speak of the One who will never forsake him or leave him. Before I left he shouted after me and said "I want to thank you for having a burden for me". It nearly brought tears to my eyes. It was a powerful experience that first night in the prison. I was so excited that I left my bible in the prison that night. To be honest the journey home went so quickly because I was thinking of what the Lord had done in the meeting.

Again, little did I know that night that in only six months time I would be entering into HMP Maghaberry every week. God was working in my life in a powerful way. The magazine "SET FREE" was being sent out every quarter. It was through this magazine that the Lord opened up another chapter in my life within this Ministry.

One morning I received a little note from HMP Wandsworth, when I read it at first I thought it was from the Chaplain there, for I had received many letters from different Chaplains over the last 6 months. It turned out to be a letter from one of the Christian inmates there. He spoke about the magazine and how effective it had been in Wandsworth. He said that they receive a lot of Christian literature into the prison but the "SET FREE" magazine was more effective because of its simplicity. This started a correspondence between William and myself. At this stage I had no idea that the Lord was going to launch this Ministry into letter writing.

As time progressed, other inmates started to write. I was involved with more over seas Ministries and through them other inmates started to write. It was then that the Ministry received a name. We decided to call it **Set Free Prison Ministries Bangor.** This made it a lot easier to correspond with inmates. The letter writing part of the ministry increased. Some weeks I could receive up to 30 letters. I started to write to Brothers and Sisters all over the world in different countries such as America, South Africa, Thailand and Egypt to name but a few. It was at around this point that there were not enough magazines to go around. So it was doubled from 1,000 copies to 2,000 copies. Again the Lord met my every need. Praise Him! Others helped with letter writing. This is a very important part of this ministry and sadly some gave up their correspondence. This can have a terrible effect on the inmates, for many are completely forsaken by family and friends and they have no one to write to them. So a letter can be like a visitor, so important it is. So for me I know the importance of letter writing and I will continue to write even if my hand starts to hurt. Over the years I have seen God move powerfully through this part of the Ministry but later on I will talk more about this.

Chapter Four

∼ God's Printed Word ∼

Many doors continued to open throughout the world. I was led by the Lord to put a small booklet together with scriptures for the inmates, something that they could carry around with them verses of scripture to help in times of need. This little red booklet proved to be a miracle. There are many stories regarding this little book, and I would like to share one of these with you.

By now, we were also involved with many prisons in Italy. It was from one of the inmates in Napoli that I received a powerful letter.

He told me that during one night in his cell he had a dream. In the dream, he said he was cleaning out the toilet in the city. He was on his hands and knees trying to clean the floor. It was then that a friend entered and handed him a package wrapped in brown paper. He took this from his friend gladly hoping that it was something that would help him in his dire need. For he was hungry and cold. He opened the parcel and it contained a bar of soap. At this point a banging on his cell door wakened him. The prison officer had called on him to awake, he wanted to see him. So he got ready and was released from his cell. He was taken into the prison officer's control room and handed a package. It was sent by me. He opened it and the first thing he saw was the little red Bible promise book. It was then that God spoke to him. He took him back to the dream. He told him that, as in his dream, the book represented the soap, and just like soap he should use it to clean himself up, with God's word applied to him he would be clean from sin in his life. Praise God what a powerful story!

Through this, Christ became real to this inmate. Many stories of inmates attending their court cases come to me. They would take the book with them and read it while they waited for sentencing. I started to hear of inmates coming to know Christ as Lord and Saviour through the magazine and booklets.

Many testimonies would be sent to me and I started to include these in the "Set Free" magazine. It was through these powerful testimonies that the inmates came to know of Christ's love towards them. I think it would only be right to include some of these powerful testimonies in this chapter.

The following testimonies show of how God can bring the inmate out of the darkness and into his glorious light.

Andrew Koroma
Bangkwang Prison
Thailand

I was born on the 26th day of September 1965 in a little village in the eastern part of Nigeria. We are predominantly farmers but unfortunately I grew up when farming was impossible in our farms.

My first decade on this earth was riddled with cruelty, genocide, inhuman killings and untold hardship. My country, Nigeria, was perpetuating an ethnic cleansing that nearly wiped away a whole tribe. It was the greatest genocide in African history. Our colonial masters slave masters, Britain supported the Muslim dominated Northern territory who massacred the Eastern part of the nation where I live and grew up. This war persists until this year and you can still see recent sporadic murdering of Christians by Muslims all over the country.

There was no peace at all over the country. To say that I've been a prisoner all my life is not an overstatement. I was a slave to poverty and the worst human rights violation. People were more interested in how to get food into their mouth than to remember morality. Both enemy and friendly soldiers randomly raped women and young girls. Robbery and looting were the norm in that area. Education and medical facilities were in a shambles until recently. Motorable roads were a rarity, but somehow the Lord saw me through all these abnormalities. What a lovely God! I eventually left for the city with the intention to ostracise myself from the poverty that clung around me. It was not easy for me either, as city life turned out to be strange and I slowly degenerated to drunkenness.

Until I came to prison I had no time to reflect on any moment of my life. It was pain, frustrations and loneliness that I encountered here that brought me to a personal relationship with Jesus. I am so ashamed that I was so dull and careless to realize and recognize the many times God was speaking to me before my arrest. I was still dangling with this decision as life in prison became harder and harder. The ongoing annihilation of my life, which my captors wrongly call rehabilitation, came upon me drastically. I tried everything in my ability to rescue myself from this dungeon but nothing worked.

I am not sure I would have called on God if I were not in prison. I couldn't believe what I began to notice in my life. It is one thing to say you believe in God when you're in great difficulties but another thing to do when things are going smoothly. The pressure inside me to find God and to rescue me was enormous. I cannot explain my desire to know him in words. Hope is the fuel of life. I was motivated and greatly encouraged as I read my Bible, especially many of the Bible heroes who successfully came through great storms, like Job I said "I myself will see him" one of my best Bible verses then was Hebrews 12:1-2. The Christian life as I begin to understand involves hard work. It requires us to give up whatever endangers our relationship with God, to run patiently and to struggle against sin with the power of the Holy Spirit. The good thing is that we don't struggle alone, and were not the first to struggle with the problems we face. (See 1 Corinthians 10:13)

The day I got saved

The turning point of my life was the day I was sentenced to spend all my life in prison. Those prison wardens have a tradition of chaining new convicts to their bed on the first day of conviction. I was wondering if they feel I just might have taken my own life because of the heavy sentence, but unknown to them I was in a different attitude entirely. Back then prisoners were massively beaten and this very night I heard strange sounds: mumbles, cries of agony. Somewhere down the long caged corridors or perhaps out in the hall? Someone was being manhandled tonight! Shaking, I covered my ears with my hands, but the screams continued on in my mind, another second I can't stand; I beat my own fist till it bleeds off the wall, tears roll down my face on my knees I fall. Why am I here? Well that's plain to see. I got into the drug's business for money. There's no reason good enough to justify what I did. Like Job, this truth was given to me in secret, as though whispered in my ear. It came in the night as others slept. Fear gripped me. I trembled and shook with terror. A spirit swept past my face. Its wind sent shivers up my spine. It stopped but I couldn't see its shape. There was a form before my eyes and a hushed voice said, "Could a mortal be just and upright before God? Can a person be pure before the creator?"

(Job 4:12-7). "By this time the wisdom I gained from my Bible studies with Charles Lourde Holmes Ministries came to mind. I heard Eliphar repeated response to Job."

"Consider the joy of those corrected by God! Don't despise the chastening of the almighty when you sin for though he wounds he also bandages. He strikes but his hands also heal. He will rescue you again and again so no evil can touch you". Job 5:17-19 (you'll notice Job is one of my Bible heroes).

Now on my knees I call on the name Jesus, by my actions I killed you, God's precious son. Forgive me please according to your promise that "if I confess my sins, you are faithful and just to forgive me and to cleanse me from every wrong". (1 John 1:9). I accept all the blame. Lord please help me, for tomorrow it may be too late. Jesus, I nailed you on a cross and rejected your name. Inside of me for the first time, I no longer feel terror as I rubbed away my tears. Outside my eyes swollen red and sore, yet inside I know Jesus, and I have begun a whole new life together and my heart is glowing. My fists are still bleeding. I really don't care. What pain can be compared with the death on the cross? For us all did you bear? So I rise up and sit on my bed and the chain rattles. So, my prison life is a prison cell and that's sad I know; but spiritually Lord, I'll walk with you, Lord wherever you lead me.

From this day on I felt a peace beyond my imagination. I can't claim that I know so much; yet. It's incredible the revelation opened to me as I seek and serve my God. The Lord revealed now to me that it is not where I am that is important to him but what I do where I am. The troubles are still all around me but the purposes are clear and direct. God comforts in all my troubles so that I can comfort others when others around me are in trouble. I will be able to give them the same comfort God has given me. (2 Cor 1:4). I call this the second stage of my Christian life. There are lots of ministries around me although I feel at times overwhelmed and paralyzed to carry on.

(To be continued). God Bless You.

Tina Terres
Inmate in Florida

I was born and raised in West Palm Beach. As a child my dad and Uncle mentally, emotionally, physically and sexually abused me. My poor Mum knew nothing was going on because she was always too busy working two and three jobs at a time to pay bills and keep us fed. My Dad just would not work. I was so alone, confused and scared; I just did not know what to do or where to go. All I knew was I had to leave.

So at the age of 13, I found myself on the streets and on drugs, not knowing any better because I never had any guidance. All I ever had was abuse and no one ever told me about God, I never knew there was a God until this time in prison. So from the age of 13 up until last year, I lived my life on the streets and on hard drugs. I knew about Satan because people would always tell me I was going straight to hell one day, but no one took the time to tell me about God.

I believed them because I knew I was a bad girl. I had to survive I also had to take care of my drug habit, so I was robbing houses, selling drugs, dancing at topless bars and prostituting myself for money. I never enjoyed my life and daily routine, but I had no choice. I had to have drugs. I knew I was going to hell, so I just did not care any more. I had no hopes, dreams, family or friends, I was lost. Satan had me in bondage, I was totally caged and alone.

One day as I was working on the streets a guy stopped and picked me up, He handed me twenty dollars, and said, all he wanted to do was talk a while. He then asked me if I knew God, I said no, does he have any good drugs? The old man told me God could give me a better high than any drug could, so of course I started asking him questions. I was totally amazed when he told me that God sent him to talk to me, to be honest, I was totally terrified because I really did not understand what God was all about. I just knew he was going to find me and send me to hell right away.

Anyway I rode around with this old man for a couple of hours, just talking then he prayed for me and dropped me off. I went to the closest dope hole and bought my dope and went to sit by the intercostal, to smoke crack. As I sat there alone, I found myself talking to God the best way I could. I remember begging him to help me. I told him I was a bad girl and I wanted to be at peace and I wanted to be taken some where so I could get off the drugs and get closer to him. I told God I wanted to be taken out of my lonely and hateful world. Well my prayer was answered soon after I was arrested again brought back here to prison and it is here I finally met Almighty Father, Praise God, he heard my cries, took me off the streets and saved my life, my soul and my spirit. I am truly blessed to be here in prison because I have God now and a new life.

I know I am going to heaven now. Praise God! See I was not the only black sheep of my family, I was a lost little lamb, until Jesus left his flock and came all the way back to save me. Sure I am in prison but I do not feel locked up. I'm totally free on the inside. I'm no longer in bondage of any kind. I am finally a FREE child of God. I will walk with Him for the rest of my life.

Leo. G. Farland
Inmate in Massachusetts

Arrested in July 1974 and sentenced to life for 2nd degree murder and armed robbery, was just the beginning of my life. What got me to this point was rebellion and a desire to get everything my own way. Yet, sometime before all this happened, the word of God had been planted deep within me. At the age of nine I was placed into an orphanage after spending some time in a juvenile detention centre for being disruptive at home. My parents could not cope with my lying, stealing and fighting. By the age of fourteen I was becoming a secret alcoholic. I was expelled from high school for hitting another student with a baseball bat in a fight.

In 1968, my parents gladly signed for me to enter the U.S. Marines, where I spent the next five and a half years. While in Vietnam I took up sinful pleasures of drugs and promiscuity and continued to drink. When I returned Stateside I brought these problems with me. In 1971 I was back home in Massachusetts and going back into the marines until I was given a discharge in 1973, for stealing a motorcycle. I got married in 1972, but we split up in 1974. I did not treat my wife very well. With no food or job in the house we fought all the time. I cheated on her and she cheated on me. One night I was going to kill her friend and I sat with my shotgun and a bottle of alcohol. Killing was on my mind but not in my heart. I passed out in my car, I was homeless, and my family had turned away from me anyway. In 1974 I was arrested for armed robbery. A church sexton was attacked and killed for a few measly dollars. There was never any excuse for what happened that day. It was wrong.

Whilst in prison I found myself deeply involved in the wrong things, trying to cope with prison life. These vices only served to push me to the edge of oblivion. I began to hunger for some sense of structure and peace to quench the fire of loneliness deep within me. I took out the Bible I had found when I first came to prison. Before long, seeds of God's word, which had been planted long ago, began to grow and take root. I began to sober up and stop taking drugs. I made a decision to receive Jesus Christ as my Lord and Saviour. Though it was not an overnight transformation, change did slowly take place. I was finally finding that peace I so desperately wanted and needed.

From 1985 to 1991 I was blessed to be in a minimum prison with no walls or fences. I got married to a wonderful lady with five children and was making good money on the prison farm. But I had left God behind those prison walls, so in 1991 I was sent back to find Him. I knew that within the darkness and depth of my Spirit and mind that I could not live without him.

In 1994 I recommitted my life to Jesus and serve Him still. If you have never considered Jesus then it is time you did. Believe me when I say that once you have Jesus in your life you will know true joy, peace, and love. Admit that you are a sinner and confess your sins to Him, believe he is Lord and receive him into your life. He will never let you down.

With more than 28 years in prison, I can tell you that there are none so bad that God won't love and forgive.

Maurice Smith
Inmate in Middlerift R S A

My name is Maurice Smith, I am 31 years old and at present serving a 30 year sentence for murder. After you've read this, some of you may wonder why I've used my real name and not another, considering my direct assault on the evil works of Satan. The reason for this is simple and is revealed in Psalm 91 (and this also goes out to the deceiver of this world Satan) I do not fear you, I am aware of you, but not afraid. I am covered in the blood of my Saviour Jesus Christ. You may try to tempt me and cause me to stumble but my eyes are firmly upon Jesus and you cannot harm me. I am now the Lord's for I was bought with a price.

I was convicted in January 1998 before the Supreme Court in east London for murder of a homeless person. This murder was occult related. At the time I was involved in forming a satanic coven of which I was to be high priest. The murder and gruesome circumstances surrounding it, was part of a sacrifice and worship service on to the father of darkness. Let me add here that I by no means wish to give any of the focus to Satan, so I will not reveal all the details of my involvement in the occult and Satanism. Suffice to say that I had been dabbling with ouija boards, Tarot cards and astrology from the age of 15 or 16, but only got seriously involved in Satanism a few years later. Anyway after my sentencing the Lord began speaking to me and after a year and some months, I finally surrendered my life to Jesus Christ along with all its dirty laundry. I was set free from the bonds, which my previous life had on me. I have grown to love the Lord more each day. I thank him for His grace and forgiveness and want you to hear these words of how great our Lord and Saviour Jesus Christ is. Praise be His wonderful name.

It was in November 2001 that I received my security clearance to enter into H.M.P. Maghaberry. Further on in this book you will be completely amazed by what you read, and you will see God's love towards the inmates. For over the next two and half years I was going to witness the supernatural power of God in a mighty way. My time to enter into Maghaberry was going to be on Friday afternoons. I stopped working overtime in work so I could enter the prison. This clearance gave me complete freedom within the prison, Praise God for this miracle, for this is something which many prisons in the British Isles do not allow. It was so good to be able to walk the wings and to sit with the men in their cells and pray with them. The Ministry was increasing all the time. The literature was starting to be used in Spain, Trinidad,

Tobago and Nigeria. God continued to bring many good Brothers and Sisters my way who were involved in other prison Ministries. To date we are involved with over 30 Ministries worldwide. The literature started to enter more of the prisons in the British Isles. To-day at least 95% of all prisons in the British Isles receive the "Set Free" magazine. You are talking of nearly 150 prisons. Tens of thousands of inmates are being reached with the good news of the Gospel. Through the Ministry, we are seeing Salvation, restoration and healing taking place in the lives of inmates. I was inspired yet again by our precious Saviour to put together another booklet with poetry and testimonies of inmates. It was called "Peace with God" and again this was a powerful little booklet. Thousands were printed and sent out to the prisons we were involved with throughout the world.

One story I will share regarding this powerful little book is as follows: - I had run out of copies and I phoned my publisher (whom I am grateful for) and asked him for another 500 copies. He told me that it would be better if I ordered 1,000 copies. My very words to him were "Well, God must want me to have 500 extra copies". So I ordered 1,000 copies. Within a few days I received a letter from one of the Chaplains of a young offender's institution in England. He had seen the "Peace with God" booklet and was so blessed by it. He said that it was coming up to Christmas and he thought it would be wonderful if each of the young lads there could receive one. He told me that the only problem was that there were 500 of them. Praise God he knew that I needed those extra 500 copies. So that Christmas 500 young offenders received a gift of "Peace with God" seeds sown in the lives of these young men. Again as always our Blessed Saviour met every need in a supernatural way. There was a large amount of money involved with this book, and as always we had been praying for this amount. Only a few days remained for me to clear the bill.

I was called to speak at a house group meeting and on the way out I was handed the exact amount to clear the bill. Once again the Lord had proved himself my provider.

Again there are many wonderful stories regarding this book - too many to mention.

Later we were blessed to see this translated into Russian and used within the prisons in the Ukraine, I will talk more about this later on.

I am completely in awe of the living God for the way he started to use this Ministry. For in only a few years he has taken me and used me to reach out to thousands of inmates throughout the world. You know, in that time many things have been thrown at me regarding Prison Ministry. One thing people advise me against is not to use my home address for mail, they say I should have a P.O. Box. You know what my answer to them is? Having a P.O. Box is trusting in the world. I am trusting in God. I have never thought about a P.O. Box. There may be a good reason for it but personally it never entered my mind. Throughout this time my relationship with Christ grew closer than ever before. He began to open up the scriptures to me in a powerful way. One night I had just read a portion of scripture. I went to put my Bible away, when God spoke to me and told me that he wanted me to read something else. He told me to open up the Bible where just shortly before I had placed a piece of paper which had fallen onto the floor. I shoved it into the Bible not having a clue where I had placed it. He told me to open it and it was Isaiah Ch 42. I read it and was completely amazed at God's words to me. In this passage it started by saying in verse one -

"Behold my servant, whom I uphold: mine elect, in whom my soul delighteth: I have put my spirit upon him: he shall bring forth judgement to the Gentiles". Verses 6 & 7 go on to say, "I, the Lord, have called thee in righteousness, and will hold thine hand, and will keep thee, and give thee for covenant of the people, for a light of the Gentiles. To open the blind eyes, to bring out the prisoners from the prison, and them that sit in darkness out of the prison house".

When I read verse 7 I was almost scared to read on, what a powerful message from the Lord! This scripture is very close to my heart and always will be. So throughout God's word he would continually speak to me about the Ministry. Many people would come and go within the Ministry. I am thankful to God for every one of them.

Earlier on in the previous chapter I spoke of the Max See Prison Zambia. This is a terrible third world prison. Food is basically non-existent. Most inmates only get a handful of meal a day. They have no basic needs such as soap, toothpaste, toothbrushes etc. Many are crammed into one cell. Disease and sickness are rife throughout the prison such as T.B. malaria, cholera and Aids are in high percentages of inmates. I started to receive mail from these inmates. As you can imagine, postage is hard to come by. They receive aerogramme letters pre-paid sometimes to write to me. Many pages could be written about the suffering in this place but I want to speak about how God is moving there. Despite the awful conditions, there are many inmates who trust Christ as their Saviour. They may be suffering physically on the outside but they have peace and rest within, through Christ. The Grace of God is upon many of them, for many are not in anyway suffering from illness. Within this prison there is a Death Row section, or the condemned section as it is known. Only recently God has moved in a powerful way, for many have been taken off the row and sentences have been reduced. Many are also being released. All through answered prayer.

At one time I was receiving letters from at least 100 inmates from this prison. As you can well imagine many letters I received were asking for help wanting money, clothes etc. At times God has made it possible to be able to help. But as I tell the Brothers there, the main aim of this Ministry is to reach out with the good news of the Gospel. Today we send out basic toiletries to the inmates there. Many families suffer as you can imagine; children cannot afford to attend school etc. The situation is bleak in Zambia, but we have a Mighty God who can move in the darkest of situations.

Medicine is an unknown commodity there and many who suffer are thrown into a cell with others who are suffering with disease. It is a blessing to share the love of Christ with these inmates. We have also been able to help some of the family members at times.

This is a letter from a Brother in Zambia: -

Max- Sec- Prison
Death Row
Zambia

13th April 2004

Dear servant of God, Martin Tuson.

I praise the Lord Jesus Christ that you're all in a remarkable state of health, which is both physically and spiritually. And lovely Christian greetings to you and your family, in the most wonderful and precious name of our good living Lord Jesus Christ. And be informed that of your kind letter dated 29th March 2004, which I received on the 9th April 2004. With praise and many thanks to the Lord Jesus Christ through you, his faithful, kind and devoted servant of him "God" to deliver his kind letter to me, a poor prisoner.

I thank you very much for your encouraging words especially at this moment of trials and persecution. I am very blessed with the words you always write to me because sometimes when I'm being taken away by my situation, I receive encouraging words that bring me closer to Jesus Christ that I only surround myself completely in the Lord. The Lord is able to give me comfort and love that no man can give but only those whose dependence is in the Lord himself who is directing them to do His will on those he wants to receive his messages.

Many thanks also for your fervent prayers you're rendering to me day and night before the precious throne of grace as this is the only way we can portray our love to each other in God's sight and also to kindly ask for physical protection, healing against any sickness. I am saying this because I really believe God is omniscient and omnipotent in everything here on this Earth in Heaven and even in the next world to come.

Therefore I thank God always for his caring hand through you, who really empathize with my situation and also who understands that I am a human being who is abound into sin at any time as I am not immune to temptation here on Earth; I will continue to pray for you and all those you work with you in your blessed Ministries for to render His Holy blessing upon you daily to the end.

Convey my Christian greetings to all those you share faith with in the Lord Jesus Christ. Once again I remain desiring to hear from you in due course.

Chapter Five

∼ First Miracle of Healing ∼

It was Nicky Cruz who stated that you see God move in the darkest of places, but this is where you will be under the most attack. The prison is the domain of the Devil and he thinks that he is in control here. One inmate wrote to me a while back and told me that what the Devil has meant for bad, the Lord has turned around and meant for good. For it was in prison that he accepted Christ. God is indeed moving powerfully through out the many prisons of the world. He is pouring out his Spirit in these last days. I have a friend and Brother in Christ who is starting to serve his 29th year in prison. He is in the USA. He has his own prison Ministry which he runs from within the prison. Leo is a blessing and it is clear to see through him that God does indeed keep his children. Many Christian inmates are serving long sentences and they feel they can't be used whilst incarcerated. But their light shines out to other inmates, also through our magazine, God can use them throughout the world as they share their testimonies. It was around the middle of

2002 that I was strongly being lead to pray for the inmates that I visited who were suffering through illness or any physical ailments.

The Lord opened up his word to me and he told me to pray for those in need physically in body. At first I did not obey, but then the Lord spoke to me through the book of ACTS Chapter 4 Verse 29 and 30. Which said -

" And now, Lord, behold their threatenings; and grant onto thy servants, that with all boldness that we may speak thy word. By stretching forth thy hand to heal: and that signs and wonders may be done by the name of thy Holy Child Jesus."

This scripture was my strength and before I would enter Maghaberry, I would read this and claim what it said. Also in Matthew's Gospel, Chapter 10 Verse 1, God used this verse to speak to me. In this verse the Lord was sending out the disciples to preach. He gave them power over all sickness, illness and demons. God told me that I was his disciple and that the power he gave to the disciples then was still available for me to day. For he is the same Yesterday, To-day and forever. So I believed what God was telling me and I remembered the very first miracle, which took place in Maghaberry. It was in the remand part of the prison. I visited a young guy Darren and we spoke and talked about the Lord. He had accepted Christ at a young age but got involved with the wrong people and ended up on drugs. He was suffering and in great pain from a back injury. I spoke to him about God's healing power, for I myself had experienced God's healing power only a few years before when I was healed from torn ligaments in my shoulder. I shared my own experience with Darren and then I prayed for him. I left and made my way over to the other houses. The following Tuesday I received a letter from Darren, this is what he said:-

Darren
Maghaberry Prison

Saturday 27th July

Dear Martin,
Thank you for coming to see me yesterday for I learned a great lot. Martin, yesterday when you were here we were talking about God healing the sick and you were telling me about your shoulder and your experience. Well, Martin, I saw God work a miracle on myself for that day my back pain just went and I could not believe it, Martin, for you said it would.

Praise God for this miracle that was the very first miracle of healing that I witnessed in Maghaberry.

I know that where the Spirit of God moves, signs, wonders and miracles will always follow. As the Apostle Paul says in the book of Thessolonians Chapter 1 Verse 5 -

"We did not only come with the word, but in power and the Holy Ghost."

In the next few years I was to witness God's healing power in an incredible way.

As you continue to read on, I will share many more of God's wonderful miracles of healing within the prison cell.

It was at this point that I started to receive mail from Egypt. One of the Brothers in Christ was called Tito.

Tito was raised in the Muslim faith and was to be trained as a Muslim Scholar. He has a powerful testimony. His parents set him up on a false drug's charge and he was sentenced to life in an Egyptian prison. This man can talk about forgiveness, for he has forgiven his family for this act. Many of the inmates who write to me are behind bars for drug related offences. Some are innocent, some are not but in the likes of Thailand and Egypt the sentence they receive is severe. Many are turning to Christ from the Muslim faith. When they do so they are ex-communicated from their families. So their situation is bleak but Praise God they have "a friend in Jesus, all their sins and griefs to bear". For they are experiencing Christ's love toward them. In one particular prison we are involved with in Cairo Egypt, many of the inmates rely on making beadwork to sell, so as they can buy food, clothing etc. with the money raised. We are helping to sell such beadwork. It is beautifully hand-crafted and they make anything from handbags to keychains and pens. Christians outside supply the materials and they are taken into the prison where the inmates will then turn them into craft wear. This is another part of this Ministry. God is indeed moving within the walls of this prison.

I started to receive many letters from the United States. Through Nicky Cruz's Outreach we got involved with some prison ministries in America. Again the prisons there are different. One Brother in Christ, Robert Smith, wrote to me from Sacramento State Prison. Robert was a Vietnam Veteran and he has an amazing testimony of how God spared his life while under attack from the Vietcon. He was called the "miracle man" by other soldiers in his regiment. The prison that he is in suffers from much gang violence. Everytime he wrote to me he would be on 24-hour lockdown due to an incident in the prison. In places like this it is hard to take your stand for Christ but he does indeed give strength. Another Brother in Christ wrote to me from Italy. He had spoken of his health problems. He had trouble with his heart. Again I have seen God touch this inmate. I wrote to him and prayed for him through the letter. He later wrote and told me that he was back playing football after 4 or 5 years and he was doing things he could not do before. We give God all of the glory yet again for touching this Brother.

Chapter Six

∽ Reaching Out ∽

Over the past few years, many inmates have written and asked me to write for a Royal Pardon, at certain times of the year a pardon would be given out especially in Thailand and Nepal. If you had told me only a few years before that I would be writing to the King of Thailand and the King of Nepal I think I would have some trouble believing you.

But this did happen one of the many strange things that I had to do, along with being asked to find old GCSE papers in French and motor mechanic volumes for two inmates! I thank God at times he made it possible for us to help inmates in a more practical way. I have a Brother in Christ whose name is Francis Ngoma. Francis was in Max Security Prison Zambia. He came to trust Christ as his Saviour at this time. He is now released and training in Zambia Bible School. He is a true man of God. Through Francis we have been able to help some of the Brothers in Mukobeko Prison (Max Sec Prison). Some money has been sent to Francis and he travelled to the prison, and purchased bread, razors, soap etc. and passed it on to the Brothers there. I want to share with you a few stories of how so little can mean so much to these inmates. One Brother had received a toothbrush from us. He saw God at work through such a small item. Even God can speak through a toothbrush. Others tell of how blessed they are to receive soap and other basic needs. One story which touched my heart, again from Zambia. I heard from another inmate who was suffering from AIDS. He wrote to thank me, for others who were going to bath and care for the sick. Just because I had helped some inmates they shared what they had with those suffering from AIDS. It would bring tears to anyone's eyes. Yet again the compassion of Christ is shining through. I started to sense again that God would move within these third world prisons. I knew that medicine was non existent, but I also knew that God was the healer. Again in later years I would witness many powerful miracles taking place in these third world countries.

Within Max Sec Prison many of the inmates decided to start their own branch of "Set free Prison Ministry". I started to receive rotas from them about members and about the time they met for prayer and worship. They even had their own chairman and secretary. Many of the families of these men suffer, sadly with wives being forced into prostitution, etc. As I said earlier Zambia is in a bad way. Hunger and death are all around. Only last year I heard of two brothers in Christ who died through illness. They both wrote to me and only recently I received a letter from one of their wives. Helen wrote and told me that she was looking through her husband's personal belongings and she found a notebook with my address in it. It had been ticked so she wrote to me. Praise God for this Sister for she is involved with visiting inmates etc. and trying to help in whatever way she can. As I stressed earlier, letter writing is an important part of this Ministry. It would be very easy for me to ignore some of the letters I receive but I will always answer and write back and show my love through Christ for the inmate. A Brother in Thailand wrote the following letter to me: -

You see people everyday come into the prison but it is very hard to see them going. I want you to know that I wrote many letters to many Ministries and Churches. I mean as many as I could get their addresses and yet, you remain the only one who had answered me. However, what you said in your letter that it may not be what I expected to hear from you, I did sympathize with you in the sense that you showed me love and concern. Naturally, I felt slumbered momentarily. Then came the power behind your words and I quote, "FROM THIS VERY DAY, FIDELIS, YOU WILL BE IN MY PRAYERS" caught my hope and energized me. Sincerely speaking, before I got your letter, I was almost at the point of no return. I mean, the prison had almost caught me up. Many so called Christians today had made me under this very situation to doubt my faith but thanks be to God who had reassured me of his mercies and love through you. Living a life without friends or family is just lifeless and now as a prisoner in Asia, I thought it wise at this point to give my life up. I am very very heavy-hearted and it is only God who could control my present situation. I know you might be surprised to hear this but I feel that the only way I could thank you properly is to let you know your letter saved my life. And this is why I want to elaborate what God did for me through your letter. I believe in God but I have not experienced his presence the way I did through mail.

Two weeks ago when our counsellor came around to see the remaining Nigerians, I was not called out and yet that only triggered my anger making me see him as inhumane. I am very sorry to say this but the truth remains the truth, a hungry man is an angry man. After his coming, my condition deteriorated completely. Your letter which I clenched a lot still has a cooling power which made it something different, it is well filed so as to re-read it anytime I feel downcast. Once again I thank you and I pray that God will give you all your heart desires. I don't know you very well but to me, you are the first true Christian I have met.

You Brother in Christ
Fidelis Okoli

I have seen many miracles regarding mail, letters arriving with no postage and letters sent from other countries with the same stamp that I had used. I received a letter from the U.S. with two first class English stamps, which had already been used. Mail gets into many Muslim countries. This is a miracle, considering their hatred towards Christianity. I started to realize that there was much need for Christian material especially Bibles, so we started to send Bibles and New Testaments out to inmates throughout the world. What a precious gift to receive the Word of God! One Bible was sent to a Sister in England in HMP Send. She said that when she opened the Bible that the Holy Spirit came upon her in a mighty way. Again I thank God for making it possible for us to post and send Bibles out to our Brothers and Sisters. It's crazy today to think of the many Bibles we have in our homes today (most never read) and yet there are many hungry for the word of God.

Chapter Seven

∼ H.M.P. Maghaberry ∼

Each Friday my time was taken up in Maghaberry prison. It is about a 70-mile round trip from my home. In March 2002 I experienced something which I will never forget. I will share what took place that Friday 27th March. As always, when I head into the prison I would seek the Lord in prayer before entering onto the wings. This day in particular I prayed and asked God to move powerfully and that I would see Salvation, restoration and healing. I committed my steps onto Him and asked Him to give me the words to speak to the inmates.

I proceeded through the normal security and went on to Erne House, the Lifer's Wing. Each house has six wings. That day I stopped with my friend Ricky. For some time I had been visiting him, sharing the love of Christ with him. I remember some months before, Ricky said to me that he wished that he was a third of the man I was, I told him that there was nothing good about me; the only good thing was Christ in my life. You know, the only difference in God's eyes between me and these guys is that I have accepted Christ and they have not. For we are all sinners and it is only by the grace of God that we are saved. This day Ricky went on to tell me that he had read a little book I had left him, about becoming a Christian. He said that it was simple to understand that when he came to the end he prayed the sinner's prayer from his heart. It took a while for my mind to register what he had just told me. I said, "Ricky, you have given your life to Christ. Praise God." He said that he did not see any flashing lights. I told him that I could prove if he was sincere. I asked him if he had done anything that had upset him recently. He said, that he was upset about this one thing in particular. I then went on to ask him how he would have felt if he had done this same thing before accepting Christ. He then understood, and said, "Martin, I would not have felt anything", so this proves that the Holy Spirit has entered in, convicting him of sin.

After I prayed with Ricky, I headed up the wing. I came across another friend of mine who had badly damaged his back in work only hours before. He was in a bad way and could barely walk. I asked him if I could pray for him. He told me that this would be OK. It took some time for him to get back to his cell. Believe me when I tell you he was in sheer agony. He gradually lowered himself onto his bed and then I prayed for him. When I had finished I asked him if he could try to do something that he could not do before. He started to move and twist from side to side. He said to me "There's something not quite right here". He then bounced onto his feet, bent over and touched his toes and started to run on the spot. Praise God he was instantly healed. He threw his arms around me and I told him that God loved him so much that he had touched him in body and I pray that a greater healing would take place within his heart. Only minutes later he was wrestling with a seventeen stone guy in the cell next to him. The following is his testimony called, "It happened to me".

IT HAPPENED TO ME

For many years I have fought and flirted with God, and verbally attacked those who proclaim any sort of faith. My reasons for these verbal assaults I'm still working on. I just wanted to test any believer, challenge them in their belief.

My day to day life is pretty much what I make it. On any given day I would be one to exercise, and keep fit. I've never known an injury that has affected me to the point of bed rest. So you can imagine how concerned I was when I damaged my back in work. My job entails manual labour; so lifting is a general every day task. On this day I picked up some light objects to place elsewhere. It had been raining and the paving slabs I was walking on were wet. One is tilted as a ramp. On walking across it my left leg shot out from under me. Though I didn't go down, I felt a piercing pain shoot through the bottom of my spine. This was like no pain I had ever felt before. I went directly to the doctor, where I couldn't even cross my legs during the examination. The doctor's opinion was that I had nipped the nerve on the disc of my lower spine. He advised me to do nothing but bed rest. The pain that I was in, there was no other issue on my mind but that, and that messed me up big time. I'm just not used to lying about the place doing nothing. I lay on my bed, and believe me I was in agony. Turning over or an attempt to get up for any reason was intense pain. This was serious, and it felt like it wasn't going away any time soon.

Later in the afternoon Martin Tuson came to see me. He'd heard that I had damaged my back. I guess it was easy to tell going by the shape I was in! He asked if he could pray for my back. I told him to BASH AWAY but to be honest, it was in my usual snide way and cynical approach that I said this. I'd heard of people being healed, and people laying on hands e.t.c, and viewed it like I did with the rest of my opinion of religion "a load of rubbish". I've always been too busy challenging people on their faith and belief to believe myself. Anyway, this guy just sits on the end of my bed and asks God to heal my back. That simple! Now this is the hard part for me. I SAT UP, AND STOOD UP. I tell you, I just got up and stretched over and touched my toes to test what he had just said, and I did so with ease. Apart from a little stiffness, all was well with my back. I couldn't believe this but believe me I was forced into believing. I had no other option but to believe what had just happened. To deny it would have been trying to deny that I had ever hurt my back in the first place, and believe me I was in agony. I try telling people what happened, and they look at me in shock, given my usual approach to matters like this. It's the hardest thing to do. Yet I am in a position for the first time in my life that I have to believe because it happened to me. It really did. Convincing others is the hardest thing to do, but it really did happen. I would be lying if I said otherwise. Now I'm the one challenged into faith, and though I'm not really too sure on what to do next, I can't ignore what happened to me.

    That night he stood in the Alpha Group and testified to God's healing power. Through this whole incident he is now walking stronger in the Lord. When I drove home that night my head was in the clouds, to witness such an awesome miracle was wonderful. Again God demonstrated His love that day. The following week, I headed back into the prison and one of the first people I met was my Brother who had been healed from his back injury. He was working out on the bags, sparring. He was hitting the bag harder than he ever hit it before. We spoke and he mentioned to me that one of the other inmates on his wing had damaged his back also. He was also in a bad way. He said to this inmate that you should let Martin pray for you for he has enough faith for the both of you. This guy was called Andy and he was a bit scared about someone praying for him. I never have laid my hands on any of the inmates. I have prayed for. Anyway later on I found Andy. He was due to be getting out that weekend for parole. He was a keen footballer and played in goals. He was upset because his friend had arranged a football match for him on the Monday. He was told it would be at least six weeks before he could do anything. I said to Andy, "What a powerful testimony to the power of God, if you could play this match on Monday." He said there was no way. I prayed for him in his cell and immediately after he told me that he felt relief. I left him and told him that I would call with him the following week.

    The following week I was on my way to see Andy, when another inmate stopped me and shouted, "You're never going to believe what happened to Andy". I said "Oh yes, I will believe it". I saw Andy and he told me that not only was his back healed but that he played the football match, saved a penalty and was awarded "man of the match". What a powerful testimony, again the Lord receives all of the Glory!

You can imagine the talk on the wings for many of the inmates knew of the injuries that the guys had and they are witnessing God's power with their own eyes.

Chapter Eight

∼ Budgies ∼

Many of the inmates have budgies in their cells and there are many times when I sit and pray with the guys that I would have a budgie land on my head or walk up and down my shoulders. One funny story, which I remember, involves a budgie that had a tendency to let the odd swear word out. I spoke to David who owned the budgie and asked him to do something for me. I wanted him to teach the bird to say two words. He agreed. "What do you want me to teach him to say?" he said. I replied that I would like the budgie to learn to say - "Praise Jesus!" He laughed, and you have to imagine this now. David was not a Christian but he turned to the budgie and started to say "Praise Jesus, Praise Jesus". I said, "David, it's great to hear you praising the Lord like that". We had a good old laugh about that. Funny thing was the same bird attacked me the following week! Another incident, which took place, was when I was praying for a guy in his cell. You would not have known there was a bird in his cell. Once I started to pray his budgie started to chirp louder and louder. Once I stopped it stopped also. One of the budgies likes to eat curry, which is served up every three weeks. While another one would lie on its back in the shower room. An incredible thing took place with one of these budgies. The story goes like this. One inmate had noticed that his budgie had damaged his leg. In fact the poor little thing got its leg trapped in the cage. It struggled so much that the leg broke. You can imagine how he felt. He told me that he held the little bird in his hands. He was tearful. He said that his mind was thinking about Christ and the fact that he healed people from their afflictions. The little bird popped its head up and then jumped out of his hand and ran up his arm. No sign of a broken leg. This really took place. It's amazing to watch these budgies fly up and down the wings.

On another Friday, whilst in the prison, I came across Gordon. He had been suffering from back and neck pain for some time. Again I asked God to move in healing power and Gordon testified to being completely healed only a few days later. Gordon says -

"I will let you know that our Prayers were answered for the healing of my neck and back. I woke up on Sunday and all the pain had left me."

Only recently I was heading on to the wings. It had been a glorious day. I stopped to chat with one of the prison officers. I said, " It's a lovely day outside". He answered, " It sure is and you and I are stuck in this place". You know in my mind the only thought that was going this is where I wanted to be. One other day I was waiting for the unlock to come through. While I was waiting I struck up a conversation with another officer. We had been talking about the flash floods in England and about the people who had their homes damaged. He said to me that it was an Act of God. Once he mentioned God that gave me a good opening. I told him that I had seen many powerful acts of God in my life and I asked him if he wanted to know the most powerful one of all. He said, "Yes, do tell". I replied, "The very fact that I am standing here right now in this prison". My time in Maghaberry each week was limited. It would go by very quickly.

My time at home increased with writing letters etc. At one point I would hear from at least 5 or 6 new inmates each week. The magazine continues to be used powerfully with many coming to the Lord through it. Within the eight pages I would always include a quiz on passages of scripture. This would get inmates interested in picking up their Bibles and searching for the answers. It was always a blessing to hand them out when I was in Magahberry. Most of the prisons we sent them to would place them in the Chapel. We had a mailing list, and we would send individual copies to inmates. At times, we would send in a batch through the actual inmates and they would distribute them on the wings. Only when I am in Glory will I ever really see the full impact of this magazine. Most of the prisons would receive 5 copies and about 40 to 50 prisons would receive up to 15 copies. I have to thank God that the Chaplains do indeed use the magazines. As far as I know there are only two prisons in the British Isles who did not want me to send them. While writing this I am about to complete issue 15. Amazing that this little magazine is reaching out throughout the world in many different prisons. It goes into at least 14 nations. Many years before the Lord spoke to me about prison Ministry I was handed a Gideon's Russian New Testament and Psalms. It was strange for I felt very drawn towards this little New Testament. The Russian Language is very complex. I was told to keep this New Testament, as it could be useful for the future.

Then when I was involved with the Lord's Ministry towards the inmate, Russia came into my mind more and more. The little book "Peace with God" was something I would have loved to see in Russian. But how do you ever start to translate this?

All things are indeed possible to those who love the Lord. Now listen to the chain of events, which made this miracle come to pass. A friend and Brother in Belarus had received an English copy of this booklet. He contacted me by e-mail and told me that a member of his congregation was going to translate it for me. Time passed and to be honest, I forgot completely about this. I then received a written copy of my booklet. It had been translated into Russian.

Unfortunately it was hand-written and that was no use. It had to be in print. I have a very dear sister in England called Louise. I thank God for her, for she has helped this Ministry in so many ways. Louise told me that in one of her church groups there was a young girl studying A-Level Russian. She told me that she would take this on as a project and try to print the written document. Well Praise God for this Sister for she did indeed complete the work and it was then checked by her tutor, who amended any mistakes. A computer was then set up and Glory to God, I received hundreds of copies from my sister Louise. Today, hundreds of these booklets have made their way into many of the prisons in the Ukraine. Yet again the hand of God was in all that took place. There are many powerful Ministries out there and you never get to know about them. Louise's Ministry "Oasis Bible Helps" is one of these Ministries. I do thank the Lord for many Brothers and Sisters that He has given me throughout the world. I would like to mention a few of these powerful people. <u>Norma Mortindale</u> lives in the Canary Islands, and she is involved with reaching out to inmates there. She has such a heart for the work. She is retired but not from the Lord's work. Norma would visit the inmates there regularly. She takes them newspapers etc. She would slip one of the "Set Free" magazines between the pages of the paper and pass them into the English speaking inmates. God is using her mightily. Then there are my precious friends the <u>Mecados</u> in California. <u>Bob and Patsy Mecado</u>, have their own prison Ministry and what a powerful Ministry! I think it would be good to share with you their testimony.

Mended vessels for the potter's use

It's difficult for people who grew up in clean and loving homes to imagine squalid poverty, or the horror of violence, fear, and physical abuse as routine childhood experiences. Bob Mecado was raised this way by alcoholics who created nightmarish and humiliating experiences for him.

Predictably, it wasn't long before peer pressure and Latino gang life provided easy access to a variety of drugs, which became the medicine for all his pain.

At the age of 12, Bob began to commit crimes of theft, burglary, forgery, and armed robbery to support his ever-increasing dependency on alcohol, cigarettes, marijuana, valium, speed, cocaine, and heroin. He spent much of his youth in detention facilities and his adult years in prisons.

Rehabilitation programs and State mental health hospitals were unsuccessful in correcting his self-destructive life style. After twenty years of barbaric mistreatment of his body and ruthless disregard for his life, he decided to end his suffering and attempted suicide. Bob spent months recovering form his injuries-and was still a junkie.

As a child, Patsy Mecado was the victim of child abuse, neglect, and gang rape. She learned to defend herself by acting tough and solving social problems with her fists. For that, she spent her youth in and out of foster homes, institutions, hospitals, and jails. By the time she was thirty years old, Patsy was a textbook case of crime, violence, and immorality. Her marriages produced three children from different fathers, who suffered through a violent childhood just as she did. By the time Bob and Patsy found each other, they were both covered in scars and had no home, no money, no car, no credit, no job, and no possessions. Neither one of them had an education or an occupation. Satan had taken everything they owned except their lives, and at that point-even Jimmy the Greek wouldn't bet these two people could ever overcome the odds against them.

The only thing they had left were the promises of Jesus Christ (luke 1:37).

He allowed them to endure years of horror and suffering to stand before you today as living proof that no one is beyond his reach. The nightmare ended and life began when Bob and Patsy discovered that Jesus Christ had a plan for their lives…just as he has for you!

Today Bob has the keys to most of the prisons in California. This means complete access in these prisons. They are both a powerful testimony of God's Grace for they were rough characters before God came into their lives.

Sister Jeannine Robinson from Missaussago, Canada, is another powerful woman of God. She also has her own letter writing Ministry "Beacon Prison Ministry". Many Ministries exist within the very prisons them selves. One of my Brothers in Middletown, South Africa runs his own Ministry from his cell. His name is Shaun. Amazingly there was only him and one other white person in a prison with black inmates. In this prison they are many evil practices including occult and Satanic worship. Praise God they stay well away from my Brothers. Again God is using him to reach out to many others there in darkness. I remember one time placing an article in the Set Free magazine. It was called, "Take your place". It is a powerfully illustrated example of Christ's love and Grace towards the inmate. It begins with an inmate walking to his death (Dead man walking) he is about to be executed by electric chair. He is placed in the chair and his hands, arms, and feet are strapped. A bag is then placed over his head. The signal is given for the execution to begin. The switch is about to be pressed when a voice shouts, "Stop". It came from the other side of the execution room. There stands Christ. He proceeds to take off the straps from the condemned man. Finally he takes the bag off his head. The inmate is startled and asks, "What's going on?" Jesus looks into the inmate's eyes and says, "You are free to go. I will take your place". He then sits in the chair as the inmate's substitute. A powerful story which I have shared whilst speaking to many inmates.

It shows the sacrifice that Jesus Christ made for each and everyone of us, when he took our punishment and died in our place. What love! Something we will never be able to fully comprehend. This is the message we are sharing with the inmates. A message that Christ loves them and that he has a plan and purpose for their life. No matter how sinful their past, there is grace, mercy, and forgiveness through Christ for the price has been paid in full. I thank God for the barriers that are coming down in the lives of many inmates.

Chapter Nine

∼ It's not easy ∼

Prison Ministry is not an easy Ministry to be involved in. In this chapter I want to share some of the hardships I have faced. One occasion, over a year ago, it all got on top of me. I was busy corresponding, visiting the prison, and ministering on the phone. As well as other jobs within the Ministry. I had arrived home from Maghaberry on Friday. That night I sat in the dining room at home. I don't remember whether I was reading my Bible or writing. Then without any warning I broke down, tears fell from my eyes. The dining room table was flooded with my tears. I had never cried like this before. I could not even talk with God. I sat and felt completely useless.

Everything came in at once. The only thing I could manage to say was, "God, please help me". You know something - when we cry out to Him he does indeed answer. In a single moment I can only describe what felt like warm oil being poured down my whole body.

Christ had touched me; I then started to feel at peace and even started to smile. He had completely lifted the burden clean off my shoulders. That night as I lay in bed, God spoke to me and told me that it was not going to be easy, but that he was with me. Again I felt such peace.

One other occasion I had been busy getting ready for work, trying at the same time to write a few letters and answer the phone. Some nights in my house the phone does not stop ringing. I walked into the living room and told Margaret that I had had enough. I left for work and whilst in the car a terrible feeling came upon me. I said, "Lord, this is not the way I usually act. I do not like this feeling. You have told me that you will help me in times of need. Help me". The battle raged on as I headed into work. It was then that I started to speak in tongues (something I usually do) but this time was different. I was shouting at the top of my voice. It continued until I reached my workplace. Then peace returned again to me. God was faithful once more and took my burdens. From time to time such feelings would arise. I remember, not so long, ago suffering from different sicknesses which I could not understand since I believe so strongly in God's healing power. I do not take medication. I completely trust in Christ for my health. Sometimes it's just so easy for us Christians to run to the doctor or go and take a tablet, instead of first seeking and asking God to heal us. On dozens of occasions I could so easily have taken a tablet but God has healed me or taken me through without the need for medicine. As I was saying, I went through a rough time and I questioned God. One thing I have to say is that, despite the way I was feeling, it did not affect the Lord's work. I was so bad one day that I almost turned the car around to come home but Praise God for the strength to continue on my way to Maghaberry. It was such a struggle that day, praying for the inmates when I felt so rough myself. When I arrived home that night I burst into tears and it was hard to hide these from my daughter Hannah. Margaret hugged me and said, "Don't cry. You are supposed to be the strong one". Praise God he took me through that difficult time. It was all for a reason but through it his grace was sufficient.

I know in the future there will be many battles and that there may be times I will get knocked off my feet, but I will be back up again, for I stand on the rock Christ Jesus.

Many people, when I talk to them, will ask me how I manage to take on the burdens of other people. It is through Christ that I can do all things. It is Christ who carries me and He in turn takes on the burdens of others for his shoulders are broad.

Chapter Ten

~ Christ's Love ~

While I talk with inmates I would often explain to them that even though they could see me physically and hear my voice that it was Christ who was speaking through me. For we know that He is here through the power of his Holy Spirit. But if He were here physically he would be sitting with them just as I am doing. Whilst on one of my visits with a guy on remand during my Friday in the prison, I spoke to him of Christ and his love towards him. I then prayed for him and got up to leave. I was only a few yards away when he shouted after me and said, "I don't understand you. Why was it when you were praying there it was as if Christ was right here with us in the cell?" I told him that it was because He was in the cell that I prayed the way I did.

I would carry around with me in my trouser pocket, two pieces of cloth one black, and one white. I would use these whilst talking with inmates to demonstrate sin and forgiveness. The black represents the sin in our lives and then when we accept Christ we are forgiven and washed white as the driven snow. Simple but effective in reaching out to inmates.

On another occasion I called to see young Andy. He was in an awful lot of pain. He was crouched over with the pain he was suffering in his shoulder. That day I knew that God was going to move in healing power. I sat with Andy and I told him that God loved him so much. I asked him what his reaction would be if God were to heal him. He couldn't answer. I then asked him if he could lift his arm in any way. He lifted it slightly and then let out a scream. I prayed and asked God to demonstrate his healing power yet again. I then asked Andy how he felt. He was almost speechless. He started to swing his arm around and then rushed past me and threw himself on to the floor. He started to do press-ups. He was healed in an instant; we gave God the Praise and the Glory. Andy had given his life to Christ at the age of 16 but had fallen away. This is a testimony he has written it also speaks of the miracle, which took place.

I was born on Belfast Shankill Road.

I was proud of where I was born and brought up. Many young people join paramilitaries and unfortunately I followed in my father's footsteps. One day at the age of 16 years old I was part of a gang that drank and took drugs and did other things God advises not to do.

Our click as we know each other grew stronger and so did our crimes, but one strange day I got this weird feeling over me, and it was God. He finally touched me and I knew he would forgive my sins. I asked a friend whom I knew from school to try and get the Lord into my heart, and he picked me up in his car and the journey began. We sat down in a small hall on The West Circular Road, and he asked me to repeat everything he said. Once I did as I was asked I got this warming feeling all over my body. It was the Lord Jesus Christ. He had forgiven my sins. Life began to go well for me. What else did I need? Nothing. I had the Lord on my side now. Believe me this was a miracle on its own. The Lord and I did not go, that was the opinion of my friends at the time. I proved them all wrong for six short months. Then bang - the Shankill Road gets ripped apart by so called Republicans. On 23rd October 1993 the IRA caused total devastation on Belfast Shankill Road. 9 innocent people lost their lives. A friend of mine was killed alongside his seven-year daughter, and wife. So I thought to myself good and hard about what I should do next. I had two options - 1) go back and ask the Lord to forgive these cowards who planted this bomb, or 2) join up and seek revenge. Unfortunately I backslid and joined up. I wanted people to pay for the loss of these lives! Our unit did terrible deeds but we believed we had a cause, and we would fight and die for it if needs be. To this day I have never asked the Lord back into my life again. Here I am eleven years later lying in a small prison cell in Ulster, doing life for a crime I did not commit. What a change for me! I have lost everything but wait until you hear this. This is a miracle from the Lord. He is still looking over me to this day and I thank him for that. As I am doing Life I have plenty of time on my hands. Well, anyway, I got this injury from bulk training in the gym. I was training flat out, and I got a trapped nerve in my deltoid. A Christian friend of mine would come in regularly and have the odd chat with me. This is Martin Tuson, a great fellow in my eyes. I asked Martin if he would pray to the Lord and ask the Lord to heal my injury. Now this injury was bad beyond belief. I could not stand up straight for at least two weeks. Martin prayed to the Lord and after the prayer and during the prayer I got this warming feeling over my body but mostly at my deltoid. I knew straight away this was the Lord and He was present in my prison cell. Now the prayer had just finished then amazingly to me, I could move my arm anyway I liked. Then I bounced down onto my hands and did a couple of press-ups. Now just the day before I tried the exact same thing. I got down on my hands to do press-ups and fell straight onto my face. Now I am a backslider and I do believe in God. I know for certain he will forgive you no matter what kind of person you are or where. The Big man up stairs works in mysterious ways, but if you are going to commit yourself to him go for it 100 percent. Don't do what I did. The Lord will forgive you no matter what.

Praise God that day Andy testified to many other inmates about God healing him. He phoned his Mum and Gran and told them also. Again what another powerful miracle within the prison cell! I remember that day when Christ touched Andy, for only minutes before I was talking with another inmate and I told him that he was going to witness a miracle and that Andy would be healed. This guy stood in awe as Andy proceeded to do more press-ups in his cell. You can imagine the effect this had on the wing.

On one other occasion I was again on the wings and I bumped into Ronnie. He was in a bad state, for he had been off work most of the week with a back injury. He was on strong painkillers. He had accepted Christ as his Saviour but over the years had fallen away. He was happy for me to pray with him. We headed towards his cell at the end of the wing. Again I prayed for him and asked God to touch him and heal him from this problem. As I always do after praying for some one I asked him how he felt. He described to me that he felt a warm sensation going from the top of his spine down towards the base of his spine. I told him to stand. Praise God he was instantly healed by the power of God. Ronnie wrote this following testimony about what took place that day.

Ronnie
Maghaberry Prison

I was having a lot of pain in my lower back on my left side, which had me off work for nearly a week, and I could hardly walk with the pain.

A brother in the Lord called Martin Tuson, called to have a chat with me and I explained to him that I was suffering a great deal of pain from my back.

Now don't get me wrong I am not a Christian I am a backslider many years ago, but I still believe there is a God out there who will one day call me back again to His flock.

Martin suggested that he would like to pray for me, and he told me that God was going to touch me, and heal you me.

Martin prayed and to be honest I felt a great sense of burning heat on my back where the pain was coming from and Praise The Lord the pain had gone.

God be with you, Ronnie

Praise the living God for yet another miracle, all of the glory and honour belongs to God for He alone is worthy. On many occasions whilst I am on the wings, inmates will tell me about the way they feel when I pray for them. Many speak of the feeling of peace. One inmate described to me that he felt as if he was being lifted out of his chair. I thank God that His presence is being manifested in such a way and in such a place. These guys are experiencing the power of the Holy Spirit.

Many of the inmates in Maghaberry have given their testimonies for the "Set Free" magazine. It is always such a blessing for me to spend some time with them. I always tell people that I would rather see one inmate come to trust in Christ, than a hundred healed in their body. For one day the body will indeed die but what we do with Christ is more important. We either refuse him or accept him. There is no middle ground. One example I would use whilst talking with an inmate would be to use the very door that is in their cell. Picture this door having only one handle. The handle is on their side; at the other side stands Christ. He will not force his way in. He will gently knock their door. You have to make that decision whether to open the door and let Christ in. It's your choice. So many barriers are put up by inmates, barriers of fear, hatred, unforgiveness, and religion. When I tell people that I am not religious or good living, I get some funny looks. "What are you then"? they will ask. "I am a child of God, born again and saved for all eternity", I will answer. As Christ says in John 14:6 that He is the way, the truth and the life, no man comes to the father accept through Him. I remember, a while back, hearing a good definition of religion. It goes like this. There was a preacher sharing the love of Christ with busy shoppers. One man stopped and shouted at the preacher, "How do you expect a man like me to know which way is the correct way? There are thousands of religions and beliefs out there".

The preacher said, "Thousands, sir, I know of only two."

"What do you mean there are only two. There is the Mormon Church, Jehovah Witnesses, Roman Catholicism, Hinduism, Muslim," and he rattled a lot more off. "Sir", the preacher said, "There are those who believe they can save themselves, and there are those who believe they need a Saviour". A simple definition. The world is crying out for the truth and yet they try to play games with God and come up with their own way to Heaven. As Christ states, He is the only way. It is Christ who bridges the gap between Man and God.

Yes, Christ loves these outcasts of society, for he spent a lot of time reaching out to them. Remember Christ spent time himself locked away in a Roman prison before he was crucified.

I have heard of many prisons being completely transformed by the power of God. On many occasions I would even give my home telephone number to inmates, I know what you are thinking, I should not do that. Well, I have and Praise God that I have. For I will share another miracle with you which took place while I spoke and prayed for an inmate on the phone. This took place in HMP Send in Surrey. I write to many female inmates there and God is really within these walls.

One of my Sisters in Christ, Nora, had been writing to me. She was from Jamaica and was incarcerated for a drug offence. She came back to Christ whilst in prison.

I received a phone call from her one afternoon. She had been telling me that she was suffering from pain in her head and down one side of her body. I lifted her before the Lord and prayed for her whilst on the phone. Praise God Nora was healed. What a powerful testimony! I have asked Nora to share some words for this book, regarding her time in prison and how God has been with her constantly in a powerful way. Nora writes: -

My Journey

There will be mountains that I will have to climb, there will be battles that I will have to fight, but how can I expect to win if I never try. I cannot give up now for I have come too far from where I started. Nobody told me the road would be easy. I do not believe He has brought me this far to leave me.

Praise God for all He has done for me. I did not think that I could come this far into my sentence but the good Lord has smiled upon me, and carried me through the greater part of it. I remember the day that I got caught in Heathrow Airport, it was the 12th June 2002. I was looking forward to going home back to my children. When I was caught I remember the last word my young son Dwayne said to me. "Mummy, where are you going?" My life was in a total mess, being in prison. My first three months in prison I was not working and I had no one to help. I could not call my family. I spent two weeks in Eastwood Park. I went to court on the 29th January and from there I was taken to Holloway. I spent two weeks there. I was then sent to Newhall. It was an eight-hour drive with no food or water. This was the worst part of my life. I stayed there for four weeks. Then I was sent back to Holloway. I did not have a good solicitor. I had no one to stand by me only God. Sadly at that time I was not thinking about Him, even though he was thinking of me. My solicitor was getting me into more trouble. She told me to plead not guilty. I did as she told me, but I did not understand. So when I was in HMP Eastwood Park some of the girls there told me to change my plea. When I went back to court I did just that and pleaded guilty. My solicitor was mad with me. She told me that I would be looking at twelve years. When I think about it I had Jesus on my side then. He was my best help then. I was sentenced to six years. They told me I must do three years. It was then when I went to HMP Newhall that I started to have faith in Jesus and I started to pray and many of my prayers were answered. I was then moved again to Holloway. From Holloway to HMP Send. There were Christians in this prison and they started to pray for me. On July 1st 2002 I gave my life to Christ. I became stronger in the Lord.

Friends, as I have done my sentence God has carried me through and I thank Him, I give Him all of the glory and honour and I will continue to worship His Holy name. Now I am going home earlier than my time. I want to encourage my Brothers and Sisters to continue your walk with the Lord, those of you who have not started your journey with Him. I pray you will to day, for He will never fail you. You know my faith was not strong but since I came to prison it has strengthened more than ever. Jesus has showed me the way to go. I am continuing my journey with the lord.

In 2003 I started to write to "Set Free Prison Ministries Bangor" and they have helped to strengthen my walk with the Lord. Brother Martin Tuson, is a man of God and he has encouraged me. When I am down I would write or call Martin and talk to him. He would pray for me over the phone. Set Free Prison Ministries Bangor has helped me so much. They bring blessing to my soul. They teach me to pray, to forgive and how to love. This Ministry means a lot to me and to so many others too. "They that wait upon the Lord shall renew their strength, they shall mount up with the wings of an eagle, and they shall run and not be weary. They shall walk and not faint." Teach me, Lord, how to wait. My friends, call on His name. He will never fail you.

Chapter Eleven

∼ Caribbean ∼

God continued to open many new doors for Set Free Prison Ministries Bangor. I had been writing to a Caribbean Brother Kevin in one of her Majesty's prisons in England. In one of his letters he gave me a few addresses to contact in Jamaica etc. So I wrote off to the Justice Department in the West Indies, and to the Minister of corrections. I received word back from them and they were interested to hear about the Ministry. Their own words were as follows, "Your Ministry is very relevant". They enclosed prison details regarding six of the main prisons in Trinidad and Tobago. One of which was a death row prison. Not many people are aware that there is a condemned prison in Trinidad.

Praise God for another wonderful opportunity to reach out to the inmates there. I sent off packages to all six of the prisons. As time elapsed I started to hear from some of the inmates from Trinidad. It was wonderful to hear from them and we were able to help out with Bibles etc. I know that some of our literature was also received in

Jamaica. I think it is so wonderful that God has opened up this door, for there are so many Caribbean inmates in the British prison system. When they return home many of them shall be involved with this Ministry. There are so many wonderful stories that I could share about Caribbean Brothers and Sisters in the Lord. Only recently I was asked if I would be Godfather to the children of one of the inmates that writes to me. Again the Lord has made it possible for us to help in a practical way. We have helped get some of the kids into school by paying for their school fees, also by helping with school uniforms, shoes etc. At times I would contact family members for the inmates. We have even seen family members receive Christ as their Saviour out in the West Indies. Many of these Brothers and Sisters are being used in a mighty way.

In one of the prisons we are involved with, we have seen over forty personal decisions to follow Christ. This is something you never hear about in Christian circles every day of the week. Many are reaching out to others in prisons across the British Isles. Again we have seen God move in healing power, touching many inmates. I will share one miracle, which took place recently. We send prayer request forms out to inmates from time to time.

Many of the Caribbean female inmates have young children at home and they miss them desperately. So many of the requests would be for them to be able to go home sooner to be united with their families. Again through the power of prayer, all of these Sisters received four and a half months off their sentences. Praise God what a miracle! One of the Sisters, Jacqueline, who writes to me, had spoke of her dismay. She was to be deported after her sentence but her family lived in the UK. She was heart broken. I told her that she would stay with her family and we prayed and trusted God for a miracle. She received her miracle and will not be deported. Many prayers are being answered. Despite the many problems they face in prison they know and feel Christ's presence within the prison walls. One thing I am sure of is that many have come to a situation whereby they have completely submitted to Christ.

For even though they are thousands of miles from home, they have the peace and rest of Christ in their lives. So many of them write to me and through my correspondence with them they know and feel that they are loved through Christ. Again it's all about the compassion of Christ.

Chapter Twelve

∼ God's Vessel ∼

I receive many letters from Chaplains, Pastors, and even Evangelists, wanting to know more about the Ministry. There are many Ministries who do reach out to the inmates but I do not know of any who are really passionate about their call. A Brother from Thailand wrote to me, whose name was Andrew Koroma. He had been arrested again to do with amphetamines. He was a Nigerian who ended up being caught on the Thai border. He received Christ into his life whilst in a Thai prison. Recently he has been deported back to a Nigerian prison. He wrote to me often. In one of his letters he had mentioned that he wanted to be involved with Prison ministry. So he contacted many Ministries to ask if he could help with their work amongst the incarcerated. He did not receive too many responses and any of the ones he did receive, were asking him what qualifications he had. I wrote back and told him that the only thing, which qualified him to be involved with Prison Ministry, was the blood of Christ, and the indwelling of God's Holy Sprit, and that it would be a blessing to have him involved with this Ministry. Andrew is indeed helping with our work there in Nigerian Prisons, reaching out to many with our literature etc. There are other Ministries who send out Bible Correspondence courses to inmates and when they have been released some have gone to Bible school and ended up Pastoring their very own church. Throughout the world, within the prison walls, Brothers and Sisters are gathering and worshipping the living God. Some have no building so they gather under trees. There is a large percentage of Muslims within the third world prisons. The Muslim faith forbids any contact with Christians, yet through the love that many Christian inmates have for them, they do see Christ and many wonderful miracles of conversion take place. For I receive many testimonies from inmates especially in Thailand who once belonged to the Muslim faith. What a wonderful thing to read their stories of conversion and yet over here in this part of the world people are so hardened to the Gospel.

Being involved with such a powerful Ministry as this, I would have many questions thrown in my face. One of these and the most asked is, "Do you think they are using Christianity to lessen their sentence?" I thank God that I can answer back and say that God would not be moving with signs, wonders and miracles following, if his Spirit was not moving in the lives of inmates for they are sincere before God. When I sit with them each week there may be laughter or tears. Some of these guys have never even had a hug. I remember one night after taking a meeting in Maghaberry, I went into a Brother's cell with one of the Chaplains. He looked up to me and then spoke to the Chaplain. He said, "Do you see this guy?" and pointed at me, "Every time he enters into a prison cell inmates are touched". It is so wonderful to be used as a vessel of God's Grace and to shine his truth and light towards those in darkness.

When at home I would spend sometimes up to three hours writing letters, mostly when I would get up in the afternoon after nightshift. Over these last few years I have written many thousands of letters. I used to keep every single letter that I received but there was not enough room to store them. A few months back I threw out over 3,500 letters. So you can see the volume of mail I receive. My postman is a member of the Ministry and he doesn't even know it! Talking about post, my local post office has received thousands of pounds from me. For I have posted many parcels throughout the world. Again God has met every financial need. Many times I would have nearly two thousand magazines to post. Over all, you are talking close to two hundred packages. It takes a vast amount of money to post, usually my bill for posting the "Set Free" magazine is round £200. This too is every three months. As my wife Margaret will tell you, God has faithfully met this need right at the appropriate time. Supernaturally he continues to meet every need of the Ministry. As I mentioned in an earlier chapter, I have never asked anyone for a single penny in the past four years. In that time God has provided over £40,000. What a miracle, Praise his Holy name! The pensioners hate to see me coming into the Post Office with all of my parcels, for they know it will take a while for me to get sorted out! I spend a lot of time in the Post Office as you can imagine. We would also send Postal Orders to inmates to help them out financially. Most inmates work within the prison and can receive a small wage anything from £5.00 to £20.00 a week.

A few years ago, God brought a wonderful Sister in the Lord into my life. Her name was Eileen Reeves and thank God for her. Eileen has her own Prison Ministry called Palm Trees. She writes to hundreds of inmates throughout Thailand and South Africa. She is married to William. I spoke earlier on about William. He was the first inmate to write to me. God brought Eileen and William together and they were married in Wandsworth Prison over a year ago. Eileen is a spiritual Mum to many inmates and she has a wonderful gift of sharing God's love. I thank God for her help; she would write all of my envelopes and place the magazines inside, then arrange to have them posted. This takes a lot of pressure off me. Eileen is seventy years of age; you would never think that. What a gift from God she really is!

Whilst walking the wings one Friday in Maghaberry I came across one of my Brothers in Christ, Trevor. Trevor had been suffering with Median nerve damage in his wrist and hand. He knows and has experienced God's healing power for many people he has prayed for over the years have been healed. I asked Trevor if I could pray for his hand. We committed this before the Lord and asked for God to stretch out his healing hand and touch him. Trevor's hand was bent inwards and he could not grip anything. After I had prayed for him I went over to him and stretched my hand towards him. I told him to squeeze my hand. He gripped my hand and squeezed hard. He told me that he could not have done that before. I thanked God and told him that I believe that his hand was getting better. I left and headed home. I only had arrived back home and the phone rang, it was my Brother in Christ. He told me "It's a miracle". He had been completely healed by the power of God. Full movement and grip was back in his hand. Trevor also wrote this testimony: -

"A day in the life of a follower of Jesus"

Dear friend,

It is my "prayer" that the God of all comfort and all Grace will Bless these words to your heart in the name of Jesus my Lord and precious Saviour.

In the Maze prison in the year of our Lord 1973 I gave my life to Jesus because a prison officer took the time to talk to me and tell me that I needed the Lord in my life and gave me a copy of the Gideon's International Bible.

Yes I was a backslider and the Lord had to allow me to be back inside again before I would come back to Him again as I came the hard way in life and He brought me back to Himself!

Just a few weeks ago, I was working on a farm on the outside of the prison walls and an old injury flared up again and I went to the prison doctor. I was told I had Median Nerve in my right wrist and my hand was bruised and bent inwards and I was also in a lot of pain.

I was put on a lot of tables and they took five x-rays. I was put on the list to see the specialist.

(John 3 V 16)

A lot of God's people have been praying for me and a Brother in the Lord, Martin Tuson, called to have a short time of fellowship with us in Erne House H.M.P. Maghaberry. When Martin looked at my right hand he said, "I want to pray with you, because I know God is going to touch you and heal you." I told these brothers in the Lord that I believed our God saves and heals to day because God has healed people that I have prayed for over the years Praise the Lord!

Martin prayed and I walked a few feet to my cell and the Lord spoke to me and said, "Trevor, I am the one who makes the crooked ways straight". Later The Lord also spoke to me again with his still small voice and said, "The Lord your God who has healed you."

My hand went back into the shape it should be, by the power of the Holy Spirit and I give to him all the honour, and all the glory and praise because He is truly a great and mighty Saviour who is worthy to be praised.

I trust the Lord will bless you and touch you and heal you and save you!

"By the blood of the Lamb"

Each Friday when I returned from prison I would always share with Margaret how the Lord had moved that day. Sometimes I would have no recollection of the 35 mile trip home because I would be in awe of how God had moved. I would share with her the miracles that took place. She would be excited to hear but she would say to me, "To actually physically witness this must be amazing." Many times I wished she had indeed been with me to witness God moving. It can be very tiring sitting with inmates and praying with them. Physically and mentally it can take its toll. When I walk the wings I am so excited that the Holy Sprit is moving through me. It's when I calm down later on that night that I am sometimes exhausted. On many occasions I have lead inmates to the Lord. There is nothing more fulfilling that to lead one of these lost souls to the Lord. Young Joe was one young man I will not forget. This day in particular I felt God direct me to this inmate. I went to ask permission to see him. The prison officer looked at me strangely. He told me that I would not be able to because young Joe had just attempted to take his own life. Humanly speaking there was no way they were going to let me in to see him. It was going to take a miracle. Yes, and God provided one, for only minutes later I was in his cell with him. He was in a double cell and his cell mate was keeping an eye on him. He was in a bit of a bad state. No doctors or medical staff had been to see him. He was 22 years old with only a few months to do and he didn't want to live. I shared my testimony with him and told him that Christ was the only one who could help him and give him peace. I prayed with him and then they took him off to the hospital to stitch him back up.

I left, but the following week I again called to see him. He told me that he was crying out for help. The previous week I had left him a copy of "Set Free". On the front cover there was a testimony of a guy who also tried to take his own life. Joe said to me, "If God can change that guy, then he could do the same for me". I lead him to the Lord that day. Peace entered into his life. Praise God. The devil is indeed at work causing many to try and take their own lives. Again I am not a counsellor by any means but the Holy Spirit gives me the correct words to use. Many miracles to day are locked behind prison doors. Sadly to day the prison population is growing. I know that those who commit crimes will have to pay for their actions, even those who have accepted Christ. But they still need to know Christ in a personal way. I think to myself sometimes that there are many people in prison who are freer through Christ, than most in the world. I know of cases where some inmates do not want to be released so they can win their cell mates for Christ.

Chapter Thirteen

~ Healing Prayer ~

One day when I got up from a few hours sleep, I went through my mail as usual. One of my Sisters in Thailand, Bongekile, had written to me. She said that many were suffering with sickness and illness in the prison she was in. This letter upset me. I said, "Lord, I know you are the one who brings healing, but what can be done for those suffering so far away". At that moment the Lord directed me to my computer. It was then that he gave me the words and scriptures to place in a prayer. A prayer for healing. This prayer was to be anointed by God himself. If I had only known the way God was going to use this all over the world to heal my Brothers and Sisters in prison! I have included this prayer in this chapter and I want to encourage any who may be reading this book who are suffering with sickness or any ailment to pray this and believe for God to move for he will touch you. MAKE IT PERSONAL. I started to send this powerful prayer out to those who were suffering. Many testimonies came back. God was moving. Many were experiencing the supernatural healing power of God.

Here are some of these testimonies: -

I praise God for His love for us. One lady here is a Muslim. She has AIDS. This sickness is very serious, but God can heal her sickness. She believed God and she accepted Jesus Christ. Since she has became a Christian her sickness has been healed, (AIDS).

Another Thai lady, who has H.I.V., is involved in our youth group here. Her boyfriend is from England. Both of them are in prison, but now she became a Christian, she is now healed, because of God. God can do everything

It is worth mentioning that the Lord is doing great miracles in our lives since we began to have healing services every Tuesday. We are all grateful to the Lord for the vision He gave us through you our blessed Brother. For the Lord is blessing us and doing great miracles among us.

The healing is still going on. There is one of our Brothers who came from Indonesia. When I saw him I told him, "Brother, I can see that you are not well," and he said, "Yes." Then I told him I have a Brother in Christ, who prayed for the sick. He is in Ireland but his prayer is here. So take this if you go to your room kneel down with faith and pray. After two days he told me that he is well. Amen thank God.

God is answering your prayers back to me. Recently I was suffering from arthritis on my knee. Now I can assure you that the prayers are really working those that you sent for me last time. Since I started praying I am now OK.

Brother Martin,
One thing, which surprised me, is that may you please reveal to me the secret, which is in true faith. You know why, Brother Martin, I have said so. It's because of the healing prayer that you sent to me. It has reviewed us a lot of things in prison including disease. So please, we need more prayers. And one thing which surprises me is that friends here have copied from that prayer which you sent. They send it outside to their relatives who are sick. Immediately they receive that prayer they are healed. That's why I said that, Brother, there is a secret in true faith.

Beloved Brother Martin,
This is to confirm that the prayer for healing which you sent to us is actually an anointed prayer from God. After making use of the prayer toward four of our Christian Brothers here who were seriously ill, but miraculously on Sunday 12th October at our Sunday Service, three of the four persons testified of totally being healed by the power of God! Praise the Lord! Our Lord is great and His Word never changes. It was also by faith and prayer that the two blind men were healed miraculously. The Bible tells me there is power in prayer! We must therefore always carry the words of God by faith and eagerness. Praise the Lord! I thank

God for the healing of the Brothers and I also thank you, Brother Martin, for your words of comfort, courage, and faith to encourage us to pray for one another and sickness for healing. With you we have today received God's Light and Healing.

Prayer is a supernatural medicine. It works through our faith and is a spiritual cure. Beloved Brother Martin, I am referring to Testimony of our new comer Brother, who has just received instant healing last week after all members of the congregation laid hands on him for a frantic prayer for healing. But the unhappy part of the testimony of this healed Brother is that he was an unbeliever for I wept concerning his critical condition of health. This Brother has been suffering critically from Tuberculosis. This Brother has been placed under intensive medical attention for the past seven months. All medical efforts to cure him prove unsuccessful; and not until last week when the Holy Spirit asked me to approach him to come to our congregation so that we shall all pray for him for healing. Everything works by the power and also the perfect will of God. This Brother was able to come to our church last week, Sunday 1st November. Then after we prayed for him that day he was taken back to the prison hospital. The next day Monday 2nd November he had emergency treatment in which he spent four days, and was given hundreds of different kinds of tablets. Miraculously Tuesday being our prayer meeting, this our Brother was able to come and give us his testimony saying that our prayer to him had really healed him and that he is no longer receiving the usual symptoms of the disease. We therefore joined him in thanking our Lord.

Thank you for your loving letter also your prayer of healing. Brother, I tell you the truth you are really a man of God you are really doing God's work. I tell you, Brother, because I can feel it in your letters. When I opened them I was feeling pain in my tummy, and from the moment I opened your letter and started to read it I felt the presence of God all over me and the pain leaving me. Thank you very much. God bless you my Brother.

Your prayer has started working here. There was a Brother who was sick and he was transferred from another prison Lard Yao Hospital and sometimes if there are too many patients they use to transfer them to buildings. So there was a Brother who was transferred to building # 5. And luckily that was the time I received your prayer and I prayed for him and he is OK. Thank God for His kindness and care.

I am experiencing the power of healing in Jesus' name. Many inmates are being delivered more especially tuberculosis patients and other kinds of disease. This has given me the courage and hope that many will be healed through the power of healing.

Brother Martin, I will try by all means to send you the results of Brothers who have been delivered but this is very difficult for someone to get the results unless he's got some funds to pay for results.

I thank you once more for the healing prayer you sent me. And the very day I received your letter, it gave me power (spiritual) because there was an outbreak of Cholera in our prison. Six inmates died of the disease on this day.

My testimony is that four of my cell members were healed after this healing prayer was read out to them and they have recovered from Cholera. It was as if you were praying for us physically.

The prayer you sent me was very helpful to me. I used it to pray every night and I can feel the healing power, because I was taking piriton tablets every evening for my body itching me in the evenings, but with the grace of the prayer I am healed in Jesus' name.

Dearest Brother Martin,

Greeting to you in the mighty name of Jesus our soon coming King. Thank you for things you send and give me. I have them. It brings blessing to my soul, and I want to let you know that I heard some good news. My son that I did not get word from for so long, I understand that he is all right. And I am waiting on the answer from the asylum people and I believe that the Lord is going to make a way for me and it's so good to trust in Jesus. I feel much better, Brother, since I started to write you and I read the healing prayer. I feel less pain, and I know that it's the healing power of our Lord. I want to keep on praising his Holy and Precious name.

Healing Prayer

Lord, I come before you now with a thankful heart. Precious Saviour, you have spoken to me about your healing power within the darkness of the prison cell. Many, Lord, are suffering in their physical bodies. Lord I write this letter now and pray for those who read it, to know your healing power upon their afflicted bodies.

Lord, I take authority over every disease and sickness, which is afflicting my Brothers and Sisters; I claim this authority with the authority you have given me as your disciple.

PSALM 103:3
WHO FORGIVETH ALL THINE INIQUITIES; AND HEALETH ALL THY DISEASES.
Lord I pray for your power to be demonstrated today, by stretching forth your healing hand and that your healing power and virtue will flow into bodies that are afflicted.

JOHN 14:12-14
VERILY, VERILY, I SAY UNTO YOU, HE THAT BELIEVETH ON ME, THE WORKS THAT I DO SHALL HE DO ALSO; AND GREATER WORKS THAN THESE HE SHALL DO; BECAUSE I GO UNTO MY FATHER. AND WHATSOEVER YOU WILL ASK IN MY NAME, THAT WILL I DO, THAT THE FATHER MAY BE GLORIFIED IN THE SON. IF YOU SHALL ASK ANYTHING IN MY NAME, I WILL DO IT.

In the name of Jesus Christ and faith in that name, I pray for healing, Lord, I speak out against this problem in the flesh.

ACTS 4:30

BY STRETCHING FORTH THINE HAND TO HEAL; AND THAT SIGNS AND WONDERS MAY BE DONE BY THE NAME OF THY HOLY CHILD JESUS.

Lord, I thank you that you have heard this prayer and I Praise you that you will bring healing through your word, for we claim this in Jesus' name. Today, Lord, your name will be glorified in this place and this will be a testimony to your power inside the prison cell. Thank-you, Lord, for your Grace and Mercy. We give you all the honour, for you alone are worthy.

Chapter Fourteen

∼ Outside the Prison Walls ∼

As I mentioned, many Brothers in Christ were writing to me from maximum security prison in Kabwe, Zambia. One of these Brothers, called Owen, had been writing for some time. At this stage I started to send the prayer of healing out to these Brothers. When Owen had written to me, he had mentioned a hospital in his letter. At first I thought this hospital was within the prison walls. It turned out that it was a hospital outside the prison where those who are seriously sick are taken for treatment. You have to be in a bad way for this to take place. I wrote to Brother Owen and told him to take the healing prayer into the hospital and use it amongst the sick. He had been attending this hospital himself. He did as I asked him to do. The next five powerful testimonies are from this hospital. One from a grandmother. Again while you read these testimonies you will see the power of God at work in lives bringing healing: -

7th March 2004

My Dearest servant,

I thank the almighty God for giving me this wonderful opportunity of writing to you. I hope and trust that my letter will find you alright both physically and spiritually.

My full name is Alice Mumba aged forty-two and a Zambian by nationality, married and have seven children. I have been suffering asthma for the last fifteen years and have been to different doctors, and African doctors around Zambia in search of proper medicine but all in vain. I used to have an attack two to three times a week.

One day, in February 2004, I went to Kabwe General Hospital to seek treatment for my disease, when I met a middle aged man by the name of Owen who later told me about your healing prayer.

This path which I have travelled is no easy road. Each mile I encounter seems to add more weight to my load. There are times when I feel I am too weak to go on. I am lost and alone and all my resilience is gone. But Jesus said that He would never leave me alone, which means he is forever by my side. Even though my way is not easy His presence cannot be denied.

Through the power and faith I have in Jesus Christ I read the healing power prayer, and the words found room in my heart and from that very day unto this time as I am writing to you, I am healed. Thank you, Lord, for your Grace and Mercy. I thank you for sending this healing prayer to your servant Owen who is a prisoner and through this healing prayer many are being healed in this Hospital.

With much love in the Lord Jesus Christ.

Alice Mumba

My name is Brenda and I am 17 years old and currently residing in a prison for girls. Like many others, I have a story of illness, pain, regret and sorrow. My hope in telling my story is to show so many like me that the pleasures in life amount to nothing if you don't have a place for God.

For the past four years of my teenage life I have spent searching for something that would satisfy my craving for excitement, adventure and carelessness.

In those years of searching, I not only found what I was looking for but also suffered the consequences of my actions. Starting with a little teenage curiosity and ending with the harsh reality of life thrown in my face.

Growing up before I was ready was one of my first punishments. I was taken out of my house at the age of 13 and I haven't returned home since. I was in and out of hospital suffering from abdominal pains.

Last August I gave up all hope of returning home. I was sent to jail for the fourth time, and was there for three months before I was sent to this prison. But something happened to me in those three months in jail that has never happened to me before. I found God.

I can not recall the exact date, but this year in February when I felt sick I was taken to the hospital and was admitted suffering from the above mentioned illness. Four days later I was visited by Owen and Robert and they prayed for me by using the healing power prayer. I had faith in the Lord, and believed that I was going to be healed through the power of the Lord Jesus. Two days later I was healed.

I thank God who has made it possible for you to send this healing prayer through your servant Owen.

God Bless you.

Brenda

22nd February 2004

My name is John Sikumba 36 years old. I am married and have three children. I work as a plumber at the Kabwe General Hospital and have worked for the period of 8 years.

For six years, I had a painful groin condition. When the condition periodically flared up, a large lump would appear, followed by sharp pains that sometimes made it difficult for me to walk or stand.

I prayed diligently to heal the problem the way I always do by turning to God. But after a few years of prayers, there just wasn't any significant progress. Disappointment and frustration set in.

Then as time wore on, I found myself basically accepting the condition in a subtle way and learning to live with it.

I realised that because I was seeking a spiritual treatment for my problem, I needed to begin with a spiritual principle.

I spent a lot of money on medication for the past six years. I even used traditional herbs, but it didn't work.

It was on this day 30th January 2004 when the almighty God healed me. Through your healing prayer I am completely healed and I thank the Almighty God for allowing you to send the healing power prayer.

Yours concerned Christian,
John Sikumba

Dear Rev Martin,
I greet you in the name Jesus Christ.

My full names are Jane Musonda Mwape aged 57 married and have four children and four grandchildren. I reside in Kabwe Zambia.

One of my grandchildren by the name of Joel has been in and out of hospital suffering from severe diarrhoea for the past year. My husband and myself have tried all sorts of medication but to no avail. Nothing had worked.

This year January, my grandchild was admitted in to the Hospital suffering from the same disease, going to the toilet every five minutes.

One day as my husband and myself went to hospital for a visit, I noticed a printed paper glued at the wall of the entrance of the hospital ward where my grandchild was being admitted. I ignored reading what was written on that paper. After four days of ignoring, the fifth day the Holy Spirit directed me to read it. It was on this day when I saw the miracle. The message was really touching in the sense that it was a healing power prayer. I told my husband about this wonderful news of healing and we started praying for my grandchild and after five days of praying, my grandchild Joel was healed from this disease.

I did find out who actually stuck the healing power prayer at the entrance of the hospital ward wall, it was Owen a prisoner and he told me more about you Rev Martin, may the almighty God bless you always.

Concerned Citizen.
Jane

Dear Martin,
In 1990 I was suffering from back problems. Medication was not able to offer me any solution. I was in a great deal of pain and wanted to die. After all I was a widower.

During this time I was visited by my friend from Kabwe. He told me about the healing power prayer. "I've heard you have been ill and I have brought you this healing power prayer," he said, "When you read it, you will be reborn."

At first I did not want to read it but since I was not at all well, I picked it up and started reading it now and again. I felt like breathing with a freshness I didn't feel before. I continued reading until I finished it. This was the greatest treasure I ever had in my house and it has become my spiritual nourishment.

As I began to read, I noticed less pain. Each word brought me relief, I even thought I would not have to spend the rest of my life in bed. I realised that healing would come as soon as I felt spiritually perfect.

I used to crawl to the bathroom. However, one night I wake up to go to the bathroom and suddenly noticed I was walking normally upright and with out pain. I started to dance with joy, and I still receive it to this day.

Jonathan Benda Jnr.

Yet again the name of Jesus Christ is to be Praised for these miracles. Within this hospital there are many receiving healing through this anointed prayer. I thank the Lord that even outside the prison walls he is moving and touching lives. On one other occasion I had received a letter from young Eddie Chikonda. I had been writing to his Brother and it was through his Brother I came to know about Eddie.

This young fellow was a powerful servant of Christ. Again I wrote to him and explained to him about the Lord's healing power through the prayer. I told him to use this within the village where he lived. Many suffered though sickness here. Young Eddie received my letter with the prayer enclosed. This is his return reply, yet again the name of Jesus Christ is to be Glorified.

Brother,
Today you have delivered people of Zambia from their prisons. Your prayer, which you sent to me, is now shining here in Zambia today. People are being delivered from their sickness and illness through your prayer, my brother. I pray that God will let us work hand in hand so that we may do the work of God up to the end of our lives.

I will soon send the photo of the first people whom I have just delivered from the time I received your prayer and I will let them write to you when sending the photo.
Eddie

I would like to mention how God even used this prayer closer to home. One Friday afternoon as I was going into Maghaberry I had collected Eileen Reeves. Eileen, as I mentioned before, was also involved with Prison Ministry through letter writing. She also would visit some of the guys in Maghaberry whom she had been writing to.

On this particular day she had a visit booked to see one of our Brothers in Christ, Andrew. I picked Eileen up from her home in Donaghadee, and we made our way up to Maghaberry Prison. I had been telling Eileen about the powerful prayer that the Lord had directed me to write and send into prisons. I had brought a copy of this prayer along for Eileen to have. Well, we had a good time of fellowship travelling the 35-mile trip up to Maghaberry. The visit was booked for 2.30 p.m., so we arrived there a good 40 minutes or so before. I would enter the prison myself on the wings from about 2.00 p.m. to 4.20 p.m. I dropped Eileen off at the visitors' centre and headed on into prison.

Whilst I was in the prison, only for a few minutes, most of the prison officers started to walk out over a dispute. So there was no way I was going to get to see any of the men. But I did not go back immediately to the visitors' centre, for I also knew that all visits would be cancelled. I spent the next 40 minutes talking with another friend in the car park. I finally went back down to the visitors' centre to pick up Eileen. I did not see any sign of her outside the centre, so I parked the car and went in. Eileen was sitting at one of the tables, and she looked up at me, I could see that she was not well. She had become very sick from the moment I dropped her off. So bad in fact that she asked a member of staff to cancel her visit with Andrew. Obviously she would not have been able to visit anyway with the strike action by the officers. She told me that she had been praying for the last 40 minutes or so, but with no change.

The first thing that came to mind was the long journey home, and there was no way Eileen would be able to travel in the state she was in. I said to her, "Have you read the healing prayer yet?" "No", she said. It had been placed in her handbag. "Read this and believe it", I said. So the next thing Eileen did was to find the prayer in her handbag and read it. She read it out loud in front of many others there. For the staff there knew she was ill. Praise God Eileen was healed after reading this. What a powerful testimony yet again! Eileen has written her own testimony about the events that took place that day.

This is her story: -

27th November 2003

Palm Trees Ministry

This is a personal testimony for the glory, Praise and Honour of God

This is about two miracle-healing events that happened on 21st November 2003

For several months Brother Martin Tuson of Set Free Prison Ministry Bangor had been sharing with me many accounts of miracle healing taking place in prison world-wide. These healings were a result of a healing prayer Martin had been inspired to write to send to the sick especially in prison but we know that others who are sick and not behind prison bars have had this prayer said over them and have been healed too. Praise God! Beloved, I can testify that on Friday 21st November by saying this prayer over myself that God healed me. Praise him Amen. This is how it all came about.

I was going with Martin to visit one of my friends in Maghaberry prison and Martin was going to visit others on the wings in their cells as he always does on Friday afternoons.

I had mentioned to Martin, that I had not seen the healing prayer that God used so powerfully at this time. So Martin said he would give me a copy, when he called for me on Friday which he did as soon as I got in his car and I put it in my bag to read later.

When we arrived at the prison Martin left me at the visitors centre, and drove on up to the prison. Unknown to Martin then, as I got out of the car I suddenly had a wave of nausea hit me. I felt very weak and disorientated, but I managed to get into the cloakroom in the centre. By then I was feeling very ill indeed and I knew I was not going to be able to get to visit my friend. When I felt I could I went to the cafeteria part and asked one of the ladies there if she would phone the prison and tell them I was ill and to cancel my visit. I hoped the message would get through in time to save my friend being brought to the visitors' room for nothing. As it turned out at 2.15 p.m. just as my message was being phoned through the prison officers walked out on strike, so at the time all visits were cancelled. I am sure you can imagine how much this upset lots of people who were there to visit their loved ones that day. By now I was feeling very ill and I had to keep going outside to get some air and back into the cloakroom but I was not sick I just felt sick and very nauseous. I knew Martin would be back for me, and knowing I felt too ill to get in his car for the long journey back, I prayed for healing but by 3.15 p.m. Martin had not returned so I thought by some miracle he had been allowed in to visit in the cells. I was sitting in the cafeteria, as near to the door as I could, and I had my head in my hands as I had been praying, and I heard Martin's voice saying, "Hello, Eileen, you didn't get your visit then." It was now 3.25 p.m. when I looked at him he could see I was ill. I told him what had happened and he asked me if I had said the prayer. Well, truth to tell I had forgotten I had it in my bag so I said no but I have been praying and that I would use it now. As I was getting the prayer out of my bag, a man came to speak to Martin. I was introduced to him, and I knew that this man had been miraculously healed one day in his cell when Martin was on a visit and had prayed for his hand to be straightened, and praise God it happened. But at that time Martin had not been inspired to write this prayer. What a joy to meet this man as I heard about his healing when it happened. Anyway Martin took him aside to speak to him and I looked at the prayer and then as I did so I made it into a personal prayer for me at that time and Praise God he answered me, beloved. The nausea left me as quickly as it had hit me and it was a wonderful testimony as the transformation in my appearance was instant. Martin told me later that he looked at me while I was saying the prayer, and he said to the man, "Eileen is saying that from the heart and she is going to be healed."

I got into Martin's car and asked for a couple of bags just in case I had need of them. You can see that I was a bit lacking in my faith even though I felt and was 100% better. Praise and thanks be to God we had a good ride home and were giving thanks to God for another miracle. Amen. Martin had told me on the way home that when he saw the state I was in, he was not looking forward to bringing me home in the car. And I said I was not looking forward to going home feeling as bad as I did. Of course Martin said, I would have got you home somehow. And I said to him Praise God you reminded me of the prayer because I had totally forgotten and so, beloved, this was the only way I was going to get home without problems in Martin's car that afternoon. God working a miracle. Praise Him.

Beloved, we know that God knows all things so God knew that we would not be in the prison that afternoon so he could have stopped us going on that journey had he wanted to do so also He knew I was going to become ill just as we arrived. He let that happen too so we know that the events of that Friday afternoon all had to happen and only God knows why. We cannot presume even to hazard a guess but I know that it all had to happen for a reason, and I am certain that good will come out of it. Please note that I had been praying for myself for over an hour off and on for God to make me better but it was only when I was reminded of the prayer in my bag, and used it that God worked the miracle and there were witnesses to it. I instantly knew that I had to write this testimony out to share it and send it out with copies of the prayer.

(What an added blessing to be able to share that Linda too was healed on the Saturday morning as you see as you read on.)

When I got to my flat I phoned a few friends to share this wonderful miracle and said I would send them a copy of the prayer with my testimony as soon as I could. One of the friends I shared with was Linda Sherrock in England. I read the prayer out to her.

On Saturday morning about 8.40 a.m. I got a call from Linda, she was feeling unwell as she has started a migraine. She asked me to say the prayer for her over the phone so I got the prayer and read it in a personal way for Linda and we hung up. At 9.30 a.m. I got a call from Linda she too had been healed Praise God.

Beloved, this is truly on anointed prayer. Brother Martin has been used by God to pray for the sick in Maghaberry prison. Many have been healed instantly or a gradual healing has taken place, but this is a calling from God on Martin's life. In Jesus he has been anointed to pray for the sick. So when he felt God was inspiring him to write a healing prayer so he could send it out to sick ones all over the world Martin was obedient and under God's inspiration the prayer was written. Praise God, He also gave Martin the scriptures to use in the prayer too.

I know that brother Martin has been so blessed by the amount of healing testimonies he has received since he sent this prayer out to the sick. God is working miracles in prison and out as people in faith are using this prayer to pray for the sick and for themselves. To God be the Glory Great things He has done and is doing and will continue to do forever. Amen.

God Bless you all.
Eileen.

I remember that Friday as we were travelling back home, we both were praising and thanking God for His grace and mercy and for His wondrous healing touch. As you have read in Eileen's testimony, she shared with others what took place and through this prayer other miracles of healing also took place.

One of Eileen's friends Linda, who was mentioned in the above testimony, has also experienced the miracle working healing power of Christ. Linda also corresponds with inmates and faithfully writes. One Saturday I had been visiting Eileen and whilst I was there Linda had phoned from England. Linda had been suffering with Fibromyalgia. Eileen handed me the phone after asking Linda if I could pray for her. I prayed for Linda and asked for the Lord to demonstrate his power and Praise His name he did and touched Linda, healing her. Linda also has another powerful testimony that I will let her share with you.

Linda writes: -

I was feeling very low and in a lot of pain. Just before Christmas I was diagnosed with Fibromyalgia.

It is an illness that effects your brain, eyes, and muscles in all your body.

On Saturday I rang Eileen and told her I was in what is described as a flare up. Eileen told me Martin was there and would I like him to pray for me. I said, "Yes, please." Martin came to the phone and asked me how I was feeling. I told him. He asked if I would like him to pray for me, again I said, "Yes, please." A little way into the prayer I began to feel a lightness in my spirit and all I wanted to do was laugh. Praise God I felt so different. The overall pain left me and I could open my eyes wide. I didn't feel down any more. All I could do was Praise God, even when I was thinking of something else I could hear my spirit praising God. The one person, other than Eileen would notice a difference in my voice would be my Mother as I phoned her and told her how I felt, so I immediately rang her and she could hear I was so happy. Praise God.

Thank-you, Martin, and Praise God for the ministry He has given you.

Love your sister in Jesus.

Linda

In 1999 I had a mammogram done, not thinking that there would be anything wrong. I was consoling another woman who had been called back.

When I got home there was a letter on the doormat from the hospital. I had to call back. I had to go and have a biopsy done.

I sat in the chair and they inserted a needle right into my breast. It had little pincers on it to grab a minute piece of tissue. This happened nineteen times, as it kept moving and they were unable to get any tissue. I was aching and sore. They let me go and asked me to make another appointment, which I did.

The surgeon sat with me, Ron and our daughter Nicola were there also. He said to me, that he thought it would be advisable to operate.

They found calcium deposits the size of nine pinheads. The surgeon went out and left the three of us to talk about it. (It would have entailed a major operation), I said I would like to wait six months and see whether it grew. Ron said, "Wait". Nicola said, "Yes, mum, wait." I thought, now if I were the surgeon's wife what would he say to her? The surgeon came back into the room and said, "Well have you made your decision?" I said, "Yes, I want to wait." I also said, "If I was your wife, what would you say to her?" He said, "I would tell her to wait six months." So we did.

I went back after six months- it was still there. It had not grown or moved. I was told not to worry and I would be recalled in three years.

I went to have a mammogram on the sixteenth of April. Before I went I phoned Martin Tuson and told him all about what had happened. Martin said, "OK. Let's pray about it." I had to wait for the letter to let me know what was going on.

I went to the doctor's and had my blood pressure checked and I asked if they had a letter.

"No," she replied.

When I got home there was a letter on the doormat. I eagerly opened it.

We do not need to see you again, as your x-ray mammogram was clear. We will see you again in three years.

Praise God, what was there, is no more. Thanks to Martin's obedience and God's healing.

Linda

Chapter Fifteen

∽ The Love of Christ ∽

At times for me it is very hard to put into words some of the wondrous things I have witnessed whilst sitting with inmates in the prison cell.

When the Apostle Paul was speaking to the Thessalonians, he said, "that we did not only come with the word but in power and the Holy Ghost". For where the spirit of God strives, signs, wonders and miracles will always follow. I wanted to share two powerful testimonies of God's love towards the unsaved inmates. Again within the walls of Maghaberry Prison, on the lifer's wing. (Most of the miracles I have witnessed have been on the wings in the lifer's house). Erne house is where God has drawn me close to. I do enter into other parts of Maghaberry but most of my time would be spent in this house. I want to talk about two inmates in particular one named Dee and the other Ben. I had been talking with a couple of my Christian Brothers in one of their cells. Dee had walked into the cell. We chatted for a few minutes and I noticed that Dee was in pain. It was a problem he had

had with his shoulder. He went on to explain to me that nothing could be done for him. Doctors and specialists over the years had no way of helping. Dee had been suffering for six years with this problem and was in great pain. Painkillers were the only thing, which he could take to ease the pain. I asked Dee if I could pray with him. Usually he would not want me to pray. He said that he would be grateful on this particular day. He had already witnessed God's power in healing toward others there on the wings. So I began to pray for those who were in the cell with me and most of all brought Dee before the Lord and asked the Lord to touch him and demonstrate his power. I told Dee to be honest with me and let me know if there was any change with his shoulder. Dee replied, "No, it's just the same, Martin". I was convinced that God had touched him because before I entered into prison that day, I had prayed and asked God to bring someone across my path who needed his healing touch and that a miracle would take place. A few minutes passed and I asked Dee once more, if he felt any change with his shoulder. He said, " It feels rather strange, as if the pain is moving from my shoulder further down my arm to my elbow". At that point I knew that the Lord had indeed touched him. Only a few minutes passed and Dee was completely healed by the power of God.

Dee writes: -

Friday 30th April 2004

I've had pain in my shoulder for nearly 6 years. I've been to see doctors and specialists, but there was nothing they could do. Today Martin prayed for me and I'm pleased to say that the pain is now away.

I have to say that when I first heard about people getting healed I didn't believe it and now <u>I'm Amazed</u>

The following week I saw Dee in the yard, he testified to being completely healed after six years of pain. The injury came about when he had been attacked in the prison six years ago, and got badly injured. I told him that God loved him so much that he touched him. I said, "Dee, just think the God of this universe who created all things, took time to visit you last week and touch you. He did not have to do that. He loves you so much he has demonstrated his love towards you". Dee was speechless he could not say anything. He admitted to me that it had been a bit frightening what took place the week before. This has been a powerful thing, which happened to Dee. It has left him in no doubt of God's love towards him, His name has been Glorified.

Through Dee's powerful testimony there was another inmate called Ben, who also had been suffering with a problem to his shoulder. Dee had spoken to Ben about the miracle, which took place the previous week. Ben had been suffering with pain for 15 years, again the doctors could not do anything for him. That day in particular Dee went to look for Ben. He found him and brought him along again into another friend's cell. I explained to Ben of God's love towards him. He said, "Martin, I believe in God". I turned to my brother in Christ, Ricky, and I said to him, "Are you ready to witness God's miracle working power again". He said, "Yes". So we committed Ben to the Lord and again prayed for healing. Before I left the wing that day only minutes later, Ben testified to God's healing power and he was completely free from his problem.

His testimony is as follows: -

My name is Ben. I am in Maghaberry Prison. For the last 15 years, I have had a shoulder injury. I have seen doctors; none of them could do anything. They only gave me painkillers. My friend Dee asked me to see Martin, who is a Christian. Martin visits this prison. I did see Martin in my friend's cell. Martin said a prayer to God and asked him to heal my shoulder. His prayer to God worked. My shoulder gives me no more pain. I can only say Martin's prayer worked.

Ben.

What love our precious Saviour has showed to Ben and Dee. You can imagine the talk amongst the inmates on the wings. God is being glorified and His power being demonstrated towards these men.

I had mentioned that when I was praying for them that I had been in a Brother's cell named Ricky. Ricky also has experienced God's healing power.

I will let Ricky explain what took place.

Hello, my name is Ricky and I am a prisoner in HMP Maghaberry. On about the 28th of January, I was doing some boxing when I hurt my wrist very badly. It was very sore for a few days until a friend named Martin, who visits me within the prison came to see me on the Friday. I told him about it and he said to me that we should pray for healing, and so we did and through faith in Jesus Christ Our Lord and Saviour my wrist was healed. I told another prisoner this and he told me about Jesus healing the paralytic in Matthew 9 verse 1-8 and that if we trust and have faith in Jesus Christ our sins are forgiven and with the Lord God on our side and within our hearts all things are possible. So may all the praise and Glory be to Him.

Amen.

Chapter Sixteen

∼ The Written Word ∼

I have written to many hundreds of inmates over these past few years. Thousands of letters have been written. When you are a man or woman behind bars many are forsaken, by their families, and friends, especially in third world countries. It is a lifeline to many to receive a letter. What more powerful a letter to receive than from a child of God. I have quite literally seen a letter save the life of a human being. One inmate, who just recently wrote to me, explained that he had written to many pastors and other Ministries and no one had written back. He told me that I was the only one who had ever responded to him. His words to me were "Brother, I have nothing that I can give you, but the only thing that I can tell you is that your letter saved my life".

This inmate was about to take his life, he could not cope with the Thai prison, and the letter arrived at the correct time for him. Many when they write tell me that they see the love of Christ through these written words.

When I receive mail, within a couple of days a reply is on its way back. I know how important it is for inmates to receive a letter, and I have seen God's power manifested through letter writing. Another Brother from a Thai prison wrote to me and asked me about the Baptism of the Holy Spirit and the gift of tongues. I wrote back and prayed through the letter that God would touch him and fill him with his Holy Spirit. He writes, "Do you know, my Brother, our God is lovely, indeed, I was interested in the gift of tongues for the past two years it has been on my mind. I speak five languages, but nothing like the Heavenly language. After reading your letter in the night, I started asking in prayer to be blessed with this gift of tongues. Praise God, my Brother, I received the Baptism with tongues following. I am not able to explain to you the thankfulness I have for your prayer. Praise God."

One of my brothers in Christ, Jason, who was serving a sentence in HMP Stafford, had been released and really looking forward to life in Christ. Sadly he got involved in crime and ended up back in prison. He wrote to me in a bad way. He could not even call me Brother. When I replied to Jason I asked if he thought God loved him any less because he was back in prison. I told him about Peter in the courtyard and how he denied Christ. Did he feel any worse than Peter would have felt? "You are my Brother, Jason, no matter what anyone says" I told him. Jason started to feel Christ draw closer to him. He said that God had reminded him of Peter and then he received my letter, which confirmed things. "Martin, I have demons in my head", he told me in his next letter. I told him to read Matthew 10:1 where Jesus sent out his disciples and he gave them power over sickness, illness, and demons. I explained to him that as a Child and disciple of Christ I had power over demons, just as I had power over sickness. "If you have demons, my Brother, then they will have to obey and come out of you in the name of Christ Jesus our Lord", I said. For demons know who I am in Christ. I told Jason to take himself off somewhere by himself and read the prayer I had sent him through the letter. In this letter I rebuked the demons that were giving him so much trouble. He wrote back and this is what he told me. "Thank you dear friend, for your gratefully received letter.

The prayer you sent to me, when I read it I felt something leaving my body out through my legs. Thank you, Brother. I want to thank you for your fellowship and prayers. I take hope from the words, but I also take heart that despite leaving prison and now being back again, you are still a comforting present friend in my life." Brother, I have good news. I am no longer consumed with anger and I am no longer tempted by drugs. As the days go by, I am becoming pristine clear. One thing I know, the only certain thing in my life is Christ. Praise God for Jason's deliverance.

Ken who was an inmate from California who had been struggling in his Christian walk, after I wrote to him he replied with these words. "Brother Martin, you are truly blessed. The Lord definitely has you in Northern Ireland for many reasons, and also spiritually here in the States. Through him, our correspondence has touched many people. I am one of them. My Brother you have been an inspiration to me, with your words of wisdom. The Lord has given you a great gift. You have helped me tremendously with my rededication to Christ . You have opened my eyes to bad choices I have made.

Ken Myint who is imprisoned in Klong Pai prison Thailand. He wrote to me after receiving my letter.

Thank you, precious Brother, for your fervent prayers for this prison. For it's through these prayers that our Lord is moving. Your prayers help to keep me going on with the Lord's work, my Brother. It was in the prison that we witnessed a mighty outpouring of God's Holy Spirit.

Another Brother in Christ there Maung Summit had also been corresponding with me for some time. I had spoken to him about God's healing power and that I believed that Christ would move there and would bring healing to those suffering. I told him to gather all the sick together and pray over them. The following extracts are taken from two of his letters to me.

27th February 2003

I have talked to some of the congregation in here, and we have mapped out 10th March for special prayers for all sick people here. And I hope this letter will reach you, before the date to enable you to join us in spirit to touch the throne of God for healing of all less privileged here.

It never occurred in my mind to do this. Thank you so much for your thoughtful advice in the right direction.

10th March 2003

My, Brother Martin, you are a prophet of our Lord Jesus Christ and our God. Christ has shown his unlimited power and resources to his people suffering with all kinds of disease. It is unbelievable, yet he has done it. We prayed as proposed, I told them before we started that Christ promised to perform miracles that day and that other Christians from Northern Ireland were praying in spirit with us. We took turns to pray, stopped, read our Bibles regarding His power he has given us and went back to pray again, to claim these powers. It was like Christ was praying through us. All sick here are healed, and we praised the Lord. Everyone left for his respective activities after begging God to continue to abide with us, after we left our Christian gathering for the day. The following day people kept coming to me, to ascertain how I managed to get this kind of power. I laughed and told them that it was the power of God and that any body who believes with his whole heart will not only do this kind of thing I did, but even more. We have started a prayer group every Wednesday to not only pray for sick people here, but people in other places with all kinds of problems. I am very happy for your guidance and believe that God talked to us through you.

What a powerful letter, what a powerful God.

Again he receives all of the Glory for this wonderful testimony.

Brother Haniff wrote to me from Death Row, in Trinidad and Tobago he writes.

Thank you for all the good work you are doing to help prisoners in Jesus' wonderful name. I feel glad to know that there are still people out there who care about prisoners. Please keep on with what you are doing towards the inmates.

Alicia writes from HMP Send in Surrey.

My Brother, you are precious to me, so I thank God for you, you are the one who helps me to stay focused. You are strong in the Lord and I am happy to have you as a Brother and friend.

Another Sister Theresa writes to me, and Praise God yet again, for His hand upon the life of a Christian inmate. Theresa says,

I can feel the Spirit of God moving all over in this prison (HMP Highpoint). Our Saviour is very wonderful and powerful. It was a joy receiving your details because I can feel the Spirit of God moving from where you are to us. God is moving in a mysterious way. Thank you, my Brother, for helping us in this prison.

I could place many letters that would fill many pages, but you can see from the examples shown how important it is to keep up with the letter writing. For a drop of ink can make a million think, the pen is indeed mightier than the sword. There is nothing more powerful in this world than a letter from a man or woman of God.

Letter writing will remain a very important part of this ministry, for through the written word there are many who come into God's presence and have been transformed by receiving a written letter. You do not often hear about those who faithfully write to inmates, and who sacrifice their time. For they are mighty people and through them God is touching inmates throughout the world.

It is so important when writing to a person that you keep up with the correspondence, for it is like a lifeline to them. Some of my friends, who have been released from prison, tell me that the letters they receive came at the times when they most needed to know of God's love towards them. So this is why I will always take the time to write to those incarcerated within the prison cell both saved and unsaved.

Chapter Seventeen

~ Salvation, Restoration and Healing ~

Over the past few years there have been many inmates who have made that personal decision to follow Christ. Hundreds have received Christ as their Saviour, while many others have come back to Christ. During this period of time I have been involved with many Chaplains. Sadly there are a few who do not do anything in trying to reach the inmates. I hear from many inmates who tell me of the many problems they face. Some of those Chaplains need an encounter with God themselves, for I know many are not truly saved. I thank the Lord for the many Chaplains who are indeed born again and who have a heart towards the inmate.

I remember a number of years ago talking with the Chaplain of Parkhurst Prison (Isle of Wight).

He said to me, "Martin, can I ask you a personal question?"

"Yes," I said.

"What were you in prison for yourself and how long did you serve?"

He thought I had been locked away. We laughed and joked about this. Many of the prisons in the British Isles are experiencing the move of God, especially in the women's prisons. It is wonderful to hear of many trusting in Christ and to keep in touch with them.

In the Set Free Magazine I started to include a tear off slip. This was a slip that inmates could fill in and send to me if they accepted Christ into their hearts. Many of these slips returned from inmates all over the British Isles and other prisons throughout the world.

God was continuing to move in healing power within the prison cell.

Many testimonies were being received about the power of God. I received many prayer requests and I thank and praise God for the many answers to prayer.

In Zambia amongst the Brothers there, God was demonstrating His mercy. Many were taken off the death row section and many were being released. I had been writing to a Brother in Zambia, his name was George. I felt within my Spirit that God would use him within a healing Ministry there in the prison. I wrote and told him this. He spoke about praying for inmates with Tuberculosis and seeing them healed.

Yet again God was demonstrating His power.

I received a powerful testimony from another Brother in Christ, Christopher, who sent me this following testimony of how his son was saved and healed by God.

I received Christ as my personal Saviour
Emmanuel Ndumba
16th November 2003

Brother Martin, this is my son Emmanuel. He received Christ as his personal Saviour. He is born again. He has believed in the mighty works of God.

My son Emmanuael was suffering from an eye infection for a long time.

He was suffering from vernal keroto conjunctivitis. Vernal keroto conjunctivitis is a reoccurring inflammation of the conjunctive, usually in both eyes, that may damage the surface of the cornea.

It causes intense itching, red watery eyes, and sensitivity to sunlight. The upper lids are mostly affected, becoming swollen and pale pink to greyish white and crusts of the conjunctive become milky white.

My son Emmanuel had the conjunctive covering the eyeball was thick and greyish; sometimes a small area of the cornea would be damaged causing pain and extreme sensitivity to sunlight.

Anti-allergy eyedrops were used and all other kinds of treatments, but this only increased pressure in the eyes, both eyes were affected. He was like a blind man without sight. He was always in a great deal of pain.

We did not know what to do. This was his condition since he was born 20 years under the torment of vernal keroto conjunctivitis.

We started prayers from November 4th to November 16th and each time he came to prison we were praying for him.

We thank God we were allowed by the authorities to pray for his healing and we continued our prayer for healing for over ten days.

It is a story of God's wonderful provisions so to tell you, my blessed brother, that my son Emmanuel is completely healed and he has himself experienced the marvellous healing power of the Lord.

Our faith in the Lord is un-measurable, and if it were not for the Grace of God I would not have been saved. But thanks be to God for sending His only son, our Lord Jesus Christ who has set us free.

I have written this on behalf of my son Emmanuel. He hopes to wait for me here in Kabwe when the Lord grants us a shelter.

G Ndumba

Franklin Okeke from Thailand was being held in Lard Yao Prison, Bangkok. He was also corresponding with me for some time. I received this letter from him on the 12th May 2003.

My beloved Brother, let me share these wonderful testimonies with you. Something happened to me that has never happened before, during our prayer meeting today. I was totally taken to the realm of the spirit and I was singing the kind of songs that I have never sung before. I was unable to say my part of our prayers because I could only continue with this praise. I could not say anything else.

My Brothers let me be and someone else took my place. This was an act of the Holy Spirit that is why I am sharing this with you.

The second powerful thing, which happened, was about healing prayers. You told us to make these prayers, and we did this two Sundays ago, and it worked. I never doubted the Sprit of God.

This was an instant miracle, generally we were blessed with good health, but there was an Indonesian man who was very old in our church. This man was sick, but was too shy to come forward for prayer. After some persuasion we prayed for him. He has been healed in Jesus' name. So join us in thanking God for His mercies and compassion. Also I thank him for using you in this wonderful way. May you continue to go from strength to strength.

Yet more wonderful news, Brother. The Asians here are one of the most stubborn people to be converted to Christianity. We started our church with 22 members, we are receiving more members each Sunday, now we are 34, Praise God. They are mostly Asians.

Thanks to our God, who has been walking before us in all we do. I tell you the Spirit of the Lord is really working in this place.

I stand in complete awe of the living God. For he was continuing to move with signs, wonders and miracles following. If I had known only a few years before the many things I would have witnessed I would have had a hard time believing it.

My life was now being submitted to Christ daily. I started to grow closer and closer to my precious Saviour.

He is continuing to use me as an instrument of Grace to reach out to those afflicted and needy men and women within the darkness of the prison cell.

Chapter Eighteen
∿ Persecuted Church ∿

We have heard of terrible and graphic stories about Brothers and Sisters who have been persecuted for their faith. Being tortured and imprisoned and many being killed for their faith. Such a high price to pay. Many Christians to day would say they do not know whether they could die for Christ. What about trying to live for Him first. In this country we have the freedom to worship and fellowship together with other believers. Yet at any sign of ridicule etc. most will run with their tails between their legs. I often think a bit of persecution in this country would not be a bad thing. We would then see who would really take their stand for Christ. I remember whilst in work one night, talking to a friend about the persecuted Church. He asked me if I were to be told to renounce my faith in Christ or suffer death, what would I do? I told him that they might as well take me out and shoot me. He said to me, "But no one is holding a gun to your head now."

One terrible story I heard about was a Russian Pastor, he had been held at gunpoint with his family and told to deny Christ. He would not do this. They then pulled out his 10-year-old daughter placed a gun to her head and told him again to deny Christ. He was about to do so, when his little 10 year old daughter looked up at him and said, "No, father, do not do this." She then lost her life. Such a barbaric and sad story but this is the reality in the world we live in to day, where you are in danger of losing your life for the sake of Christ.

The time will come when in our own country you will be told to stop talking about Christ and Him crucified. Yet despite the persecution, the church stands strong. Many of those who have been involved with torturing Christians have been converted themselves when they see the love their victims have for them through Christ. I received a prayer news sheet once from another Brother in Christ, Bob Spratt. He is involved with a ministry called "Missions to Prisons".

In this Newsletter it talked about one of our Christian Brothers in Christ, Tadessa. This true story took place in Ethiopia. Brother Tadessa had been imprisoned for his faith and badly tortured. He sang Praises to God whilst he was being beaten. They finally lost patience with him and the commanding officer gave permission for him to be executed by firing squad. He was taken out and placed in front of a wall. The command was given to shoot him. But God had other plans for Tadessa. He put an invisible shield around him and not one of the bullets touched him. At witnessing the power of God the commanding Officer fell to his knees and repented and accepted Christ.

Tadessa to day is a Church Planter. A powerful story of deliverance.

We have had the privilege in the past to write to many of our persecuted Brothers and Sisters who are being imprisoned for their faith. We have to be very careful when writing to them. There are many restrictions. If the names Jesus or God are seen on our letters, they could face more punishment. So the letters are mostly written on picture postcards and worded in a way that they will understand they have others praying for them. Of course it is almost impossible for them to write back. Again another powerful way in which letter writing can be a valued and important Ministry. Praise God. Despite the persecution many are facing, the truth and light of the gospel is still shining through, dispelling the darkness.

Chapter Nineteen

⁓ Grace of God ⁓

In to day's society especially within the church, there is not an awful lot of grace towards the inmate. I suppose even before God called me to do this Ministry I could have put my hand up also regarding this issue, not having much grace myself. But as God touched me that night 4 years ago he opened my eyes to those incarcerated men and women.

I used a powerful illustration of this in one of the "Set Free" magazines. Ben had just recently been saved whilst in prison. The light of the gospel awakened him and he was truly born into God's Kingdom. On his release he was so energetic towards attending his local church. He dressed himself up and arrived at the church in good time. He sat up at the front, he was only there a few minutes when he was approached by a smart elderly looking gentleman. This man told him if he wouldn't mind sitting at the back of the church,(away from all the good people). Ben was happy to oblige, thinking he had sat on someone's seat who sat there each week. Anyway the service commenced and throughout the service Ben felt a bit awkward and uneasy. As if the Minister himself was preaching straight through him. After the service Ben was approached by the elderly gentleman and the Minister. He was kindly told not to come back as they had been aware that he was just released from prison. Ben was so pleased and happy with himself. He walked out with a spring in his step. Why was he so happy? He was asked this very question by a young lady in the congregation. "Oh," he said, "I do not want to go anywhere where Christ is not present".

There was not a lot of grace there for Ben, but what an excellent answer he gave to the young lady.

I received a letter from Thailand, it was from another one of my Christian Brothers.

He said in his letter.

Dearest Brother Martin, I must confess being in communication links with many other clergymen and pastors. None of them have ever embraced me, just like the way you have. Your humanitarian love to me has really clarified that no matter what, there are still righteous and worthy men of God on earth. For the words that proceed out of your mouth have automatically quenched my thirst for righteousness. I confess that I am impressed to hear of your faith in the Lord Jesus Christ, for it is really a great honour for you to be God's steward as you are to day. For you have been created in Christ Jesus for a walk of faith that will change the world.

What an encouraging letter to receive from this Brother in the Lord. God does indeed move in mysterious ways.

This next letter that you will read shows this. (Again from Thai Prison).

On the 14th of May, being a Friday, I was in the midst of my fellow inmates and believers, singing praises to God. After our worship one of the inmates asked if we would pray for his ill friend another inmate who was suffering from haemorrhaging. He needed surgery but could not afford to pay for the operation. The next day we called him to pray for him. Then at 3.00 p.m. I received your letter. I was in my cell with four other inmates. When I read your letter, I decided to do what you asked me to do in your message. I told the sick inmate that if he believes the prayer that you sent then he would be healed. To my surprise this inmate asked if he could take this prayer. He could not speak English or read English. You know what happened, my Brother? To day from an unknown sponsor his bill for the operation has been paid and right now he is being operated on. He has been healed. Praise God.

Martin, you surprised me from your first letter, I knew that you are not an ordinary man. This guy who has been operated on told me to write to you and thank you. We believe that through this he will come to know Christ in his life.

This inmate has been clearly spoken to by the Lord, He was not healed supernaturally by the power of God, but it was still a miracle that he had an unknown person pay for his operation. I believe that this has spoken more to this inmate than if he had been healed instantly. Yet again God moving in a mysterious way. I stand in complete awe of the living God, for there are times especially when I witness His power with my own eyes so much so that I am speechless. (Some would find that hard to believe). Words cannot describe what I am witnessing. But this is abundant life in Christ and these things should be normal things in Christian circles.

Chapter Twenty

∼ Water into Wine ∼

What I am about to share with you may bring mixed reactions, but I want to state at the very beginning that it is completely true. Do we not serve a God of the miraculous? Some while back when I first started to walk the wings, I came across an inmate who was going through his trial. It was for a serious crime. I had been spending a lot of time with this particular inmate. One of the days I was with him in his cell he shared with me something so incredible that took place the previous evening.

He went on to tell me the following.

Martin, something strange yet wonderful took place yesterday. The Lord has worked a miracle towards me. Yesterday before lock up I lifted an empty 2-litre bottle of lemonade. I filled the bottom with some blackcurrant cordial. I then went to fill it up with water. My neighbouring cell mate witnessed me doing this. I filled it to the very top, placed the lid back on and put it on my cell floor. We were then locked in, and I got down to a time of prayer before God. I was going through my case, Martin, as you know. I lifted my situation before God. (This inmate accepted Christ whilst in prison on remand). I got very thirsty all of a sudden and reached down for the bottle of juice I had only minutes before filled. Martin, I took a drink and it had turned into wine. When I opened the bottle it fizzed, and you can imagine my shock and surprise. When we were unlocked I shared what had taken place with my friend in the next cell. He took a drink also and was completely amazed.

"I wish he had have done that for me," was his reaction.

I was then handed this bottle to test what had just been said. Yes, it was indeed wine. Others there also witnessed this miracle. Now I know what some of you are thinking. But why does this sound so incredible? It happened and I knew that one-day I would share this with others. God drew close to this inmate through this miracle and it showed his love towards him. He told me that he would only ever take a few sips. The friend in the next cell was spoken to by witnessing this miracle, and through it rededicated his life back to Christ. Throughout the trial this inmate experienced the peace of God and when he stood on the dock he told me that he could have told the judge and jury that he was now a born again Christian. He would not do this, he told me that the Lord had already been judged in his place and he was not going to use him in this way. He was sentenced to life imprisonment and while so many others around him wept, he remained completely at peace. What a powerful God we serve!

What a wonderful testimony.

For those who disbelieve this, then the problem is with yourself. For I have seen God move within Maghaberry prison in so many amazing ways. For there are miracles taking place there that have never happened before in the prisons in N. Ireland. That shows and tells me that God is pouring out his Spirit like never before in these last days within the prison cell. I cannot deny what I am seeing not just here in N. Ireland but throughout the prisons of this world. You can imagine some of the looks people give me. They think I am a bit of a nut case or mad. Praise God I am nuts about the Lord and mad about him. You know something, many people want proof; they want God to show Himself.

I remember whilst speaking in Magilligain a young inmate shouted at me and said to me, *"Prove that God exists"*. I turned to him and boldly said, "Why don't you ask God to prove Himself to you?" He then stated that he was frightened too, incase something happened. Crazy, isn't it? I know that there are many people who if they even witnessed a miracle, they still would not believe and accept Christ for who he says he is. The inmate we spoke of above struggles in his faith like many of us but as I was asking him for permission to write this, he admitted that he knows and feels God's presence constantly with him.

Through the week I make many trips down to the Post Office, either for stamps or posting Bibles etc.

Again I have to thank the Lord for meeting all of these needs. For postage, especially packages can be very expensive to send out to the likes of Thailand and Egypt etc. We send toiletries out to the Brothers in Zambia and they are so gratefully received. When I decided to start sending basic needs out, I said, "Lord," I need the resources to buy these items". Within days a friend and Brother of mine arrived at my doorstep with two bags full of toiletries. Praise God again for his provisions. As I have stated, I trust in Christ to meet my every need. At times your faith can indeed be stretched. On one occasion some more literature had been ordered. I needed a large amount to clear my bill. One week passed, then two weeks. It came to the end of the third week and I started to be slightly concerned. I still trusted in God, I needed to pay this bill within a couple of days. Well, I said, "Lord I know that my own wages will be going into the bank so I did not care if I used my own money that was for my own outgoings". Within a day or so of making this decision the Lord blessed me with more than I needed to clear the bill. Yet again he remained faithful to me.

One other time I had many packages sitting to be posted and I badly needed to purchase stamps. I had no money at all but yet I told my wife Margaret that I was going to go to the Post Office that night. Within a space of two hours again my need was met in a supernatural way. Every three months when our Magazine is printed and posted, God meets every single penny. There are so many miracles regarding finances and God has blessed us so much. For he knows what I need before I even ask. Many people including Christians would ask where I receive help. Silly question really to ask me especially from a Christian. My help comes from the Lord. You would be completely amazed at the amount he has supplied over these last few years and every single penny without stretching my hand out to anyone. Praise him once more for all of his faithfulness in this area. When you put your complete trust in Christ he will indeed meet your every need. To the very time of writing this book, there have been well over 32,000 pieces of literature sent out to inmates, prisons, and other Ministries throughout the world.

What a testimony of God's power so many seeds are being sowed in the lives of inmates, and through the "Set Free" magazine many are accepting Christ into their lives. There have been hundreds of personal decisions to accept Christ. Through this Ministry God has even reached out to family members. I will share with you the story of Dee.

One day as I was going through my mail, I opened a letter from Richard in Scotland. He had written to me because he had read a poem in another prison magazine, which I had written some time before. It turned out he had married whilst in prison. His wife Dee had many years ago lived in N. Ireland so he thought it would be nice for me to contact her sometime. He gave me her phone number and address. I told him that I would phone. Richard was not a Christian nor was Dee. So I phoned as I promised and spoke with Dee on the phone. I introduced myself and explained that her husband wanted me to contact her. I spoke a bit about the ministry etc. and my own life, when I accepted Christ etc. I found out later on that when I spoke to Dee about Christ she became very tearful. She had been brought up in a Roman Catholic environment and attended chapel.

Dee had no understanding of Christ and how he had died for her. I told her that when he knocked on the door of her heart, that she should let him in. Then one morning, only a few months later, I was about to travel up to Maghaberry, when I switched my mobile phone on. A message had been left. It had been at 1.20 a.m. in the early hours of the morning. It was Dee. So I phoned back and Praise God she told me that at this time she received Christ into her heart and life. What a wonderful thing to find out! Later she told me that when she first spoke to me she thought I was a "Bible Basher".

Praise God Dee is doing well with the Lord, and only recently her young son has also accepted Christ.

A wonderful story indeed. One other time I received a personal decision form from a prison officer in England and on another occasion the brother of one of the inmates I had been writing to, from Jamaica also sent me a form and received Christ. Through these returned forms, we remember our new family members in prayer.

Dee has also experienced God's healing power through the prayer of healing. She had been suffering with tennis elbow for many years and I had sent her a copy of the prayer. She prayed it, believed it, and was healed.

Her testimony is as follows: -

I have had tennis elbow for many years, over the last year it has got gradually worse. I became a Christian on the 17th October 2003. I had been talking to Brother Martin and telling him the problem with my elbow. On that day the pain was intense, so I was about to take some painkillers. Martin had previously sent me the prayer for healing and told me to read this and believe what it said. To be honest I did neither. I did not take a tablet or read the prayer. Over the next few days my elbow became much worse. I sat by the kitchen window as usual with a cup of tea and out of the corner of my eye I noticed Brother Martin's wee healing prayer. So I picked it up and read it, rubbing my elbow at the same time. I then went on to do my daily chores. That weekend I desperately needed fire wood for my coal fire. I had been given a bundle of this from an elderly neighbour. Another neighbour lent me a saw. I started to saw the wood, some large pieces, and some small pieces. I was really sawing. As I was sawing away my son shouted out, "A cup of tea, Ma?" I replied "No darling, I am on a roll here and there might be snow tomorrow".

Eventually I got through my last piece of wood. I filled four sacks full. I couldn't believe it. I had cleared the lot. I looked up at the clock I had missed my breakfast and lunch. I had worked for four and a half-hours solid, and better still was also given a heap of conifer tree trunks and spent four hours sawing through them. My elbow was healed and I had no pain. I felt like I could saw my way to Heaven.

For the healing prayer to work you must have faith, you have to believe. I had Brother Martin Tuson who believed in me. My faith in Christ is new to me. if I have doubts or do not understand things about Christianity or the word of God, Martin is only a phone call away and he is only too glad to help. So I thank God for my Brother in Christ and his powerful prayer.

Chapter Twenty-one

∼ God's Handwriting ∼

There is power in the written word as you have read in previous pages of this book. When I started to receive mail from Chaplains etc and inmates themselves, I would always keep the letters that they sent. As time progressed it became impossible to store them all. So I decided to get rid of them and place them in the re-cycle bin which we had just received. I believe that I put over three and a half thousand letters into this bin. I kept some of the letters I had been sent, especially the ones that spoke of Christ's healing power etc. You can imagine the room these letters would take up.

As I sit each day and correspond with the inmates who write to me, I have never once been stuck for words. For through the power of the Holy Spirit the Lord gives me the very words. When I start my letters off, I will always, begin with the words 'Beloved' or 'Precious'. This in itself ministers to the inmate, over these last few years, the Lord has used me to strengthen and encourage my Brothers and Sisters in their faith.

I have included some extracts taken from these letters that I have been sent.

* * *

Thank you for your blessed letter and for your prayer. I know that prayer is good and I know that God answers our prayers because I can feel your prayer at times.

* * *

I received your prayer of Blessing and I am so glad to hear from you. Your letter is a joy to me. When I read it, I get closer to God.

* * *

Martin, every letter I receive from you, I feel the blessing, the power and the strength of God in your words. This helps me to push a little further and be made stronger in the Spirit of God.

* * *

Martin, thank-you for praying for me. You are a blessed man and I know that God will show you many things that are happening in this world. I know and believe that prayer is powerful. Martin, your prayer for me has been answered. I am not going to be deported but will remain with my family here.

* * *

I was happy to get your letter, when I read it, I felt that it had brought me closer to God and gave me peace of mind.

* * *

I have received your letter, Brother. It always brings joy to my soul when I hear from you through the written word.

*   *   *

Brother Martin, I can feel your prayer. I am not feeling any pain at the moment. God Bless the day when I started writing to you.

*   *   *

It was a blessing receiving your letter. Sometimes I start to feel insecure, but once I got your letter, the word of your mouth started to advise me of being perfectly secure in the Lord. I mean the word of your mouth is evidently anointed. Your word is light from Heaven.

*   *   *

I thank you so very much for your Spiritual, uplifting letter. Martin, you project a whole lot of spiritual and human understanding. I am so blessed to have you around, especially now.

*   *   *

As you can see from these extracts, God does indeed move through the pen. It is also important that these Brothers and Sisters receive mail regularly.

There are not too many who faithfully write, for in the past I have experienced people who have stopped their correspondence, leaving the inmate upset and worried. I write faithfully to the Brothers in Zambia and Thailand and it encourages them and builds them up in the word of

God. At one point I was writing to well over two hundred inmates throughout the world. It's a good job they did not write all at once. Each day I look forward to reading my mail from around the world and to hear of God's move within the prison cell. You most definitely have to be called by God to be involved with letter writing. Praise God for the strength he gives to fulfil this very important task.

Chapter Twenty-two

∼ Reaching Out ∼

When I travel up to HMP Maghaberry I am always there a good 30 to 40 minutes before unlock. The reason for this is because I will always spend time reaching out to others involved in the prison. Whether it is a prison officer, member of staff, or even a Chaplain.

On one occasion I entered the visitors' area, where family members etc, pass through before their allocated visits. I was looking for some information, so I asked the S.O. (Superior Officer). She was not in very good form. I could see she was upset. I spoke with her for a few minutes and headed on into the main part of the prison. A few weeks later I again bumped into her. She told me that the day she had seen me a few weeks before, was a day where she was about to explode, "When you started to talk to me, I calmed down", were her words. "I would have lost it if you had'nt come in when you did, Martin".

I found out she was a backslider and she admitted to me that God had brought me along to remind her of His love towards her. I prayed with her and through this time spent with her, God really ministered into her life.

God would always bring someone along my path, and each week I would find myself reaching out with the love of Christ to someone. Back on the wings one Friday I came across an inmate who had been suffering with a problem in his eyes. He had no relief from the pain and stinging he was experiencing. I noticed also that his wrist was strapped. He had damaged this also. I asked him if I could pray for God to touch him. We proceeded into his cell, which he was just in the process of painting. He was a Christian and I shared with him what God had been doing on the wings regarding His healing power. I prayed and asked him how he felt, he looked at me and started to blink his eyes. "The pain and stinging are going, Martin". I then grabbed his wrist and squeezed it hard. "What about your wrist I asked?" He looked at me in complete shock. No pain at all. I told him to take the strapping off. He had full movement. I placed the strapping in the bin, and told him there was no more need for him to wear it. Again I told him to point to the part of his wrist which was giving him the most problems. He pointed to that area, with my thumb I pressed down hard. Nothing, he was instantly healed and completely amazed. Praise God for another testimony to the power of God.

Yet again the love of Christ was being poured out towards the inmate, and His name was being lifted high. It is so wonderful to witness God moving in this way especially within the darkness of the prison cell. It would bring you to tears to sense and experience this. What love Christ would demonstrate towards these guys by touching them in this way! When I witness such miracles sometimes my head would be in the clouds. At times the whole 35-mile trip home to Bangor would be a complete blur, as I am completely in awe of what I have just witnessed. I would arrive home and let Margaret know what had taken place that day. My head would stay in the clouds most of the night. This is the power of God unto salvation. The greatest thing ever witnessed within the prison cell, is when an inmate accepts Christ into his heart and life. I thank God that he has used me in this way. Many barriers exist in the inmate's life. Barriers of hatred, anger, unforgiveness and religion. Praise God that he is in the business of knocking these barriers down.

There are many times when I speak with an inmate and I will say to him that the time for me talking has stopped. For there is nothing more that can be said. They know what they have to do. Many of the inmates have Christian relatives and friends praying for them. The number of times I have sat with them and they have spoken of a Christian family member.

Over the past few years many funny things have taken place. When I enter the wings I have to wait for the door to be opened. On a few occasions I have not closed it properly and was given a polite ticking off.

When I first started to enter Maghaberry, I had been in only a few weeks and I got a bit lost. I was walking into the wrong areas and taking wrong turns. The prison officers had a good laugh at me. I remember being in a hurry one day. It was quite a walk from the remand house to the sentenced house. Dogs would patrol the prison with their handlers. I just pictured myself running with a couple of large German shepherds in hot pursuit. So I decided to walk quickly to save me ending up with a lump being taken out of me.

A funny thing took place as I was heading out of the prison one Saturday. When an incident takes place in the prison, everything comes to a stop. You can't proceed to leave the prison until the all clear is given.

On this particular day the alarm went off in the search area. I was stuck with three prison officers. They knew that I was a Christian from my Bible, which I carried. One of the officers looked at me and said, "I think we are going to be stuck here for a while and it's tea time. Could you do anything with a few sandwiches and a chocolate biscuit?" We all had a good laugh about this.

Many times I will be locked in a cell and forgotten about. It's funny sometimes to see the look on some of the inmates' faces. They seem to be more concerned about this than I am.

One other unforgettable thing took place. I had been talking with a few inmates in one of their cells. As you can imagine there is not a lot of room. Another Brother in Christ entered the cell. There was no where for him to sit so he sat on the toilet. Suddenly there was a loud bang we all ducked. I thought someone was firing a gun. It turned out to be a cracked toilet seat; this guy was a bit heavy and when he sat down the toilet seat cracked. It was a really funny situation. Apparently he had broken three toilet seats in the space of one week!

I would be offered the odd cup of coffee or tea by the guys. One time I accepted. It was so funny to watch. It took four inmates to make it. One looked for some milk, another the tea bags, another the water and the other for the sugar. They were bumping into each other in the process.

Many memories like this will never leave me.

All the inmates I visit are precious to God, but sadly in today's society, people do not want to hear this. They are indeed sinners they are in prison for terrible acts, which they have committed. They have to pay the price for their crime. We do reap what we sow. Unfortunately when people (even Christians) talk about sin they tend to put it into different categories, "I am bad, but I'm not that bad", they say. With God sin is sin. "For all have sinned and fallen short of God's Glory".

"There are none righteous, no not one".

Remember the story about the religious leader praying in the street. He made sure everyone heard him praying, and in the corner there was a sinner praying from his heart saying, "Father, forgive me". It was the one greater in sin that went away justified. We can not fathom the depth of grace Christ has for the inmate. Many I talk with cannot even forgive themselves for their actions. Praise God his wondrous love is being shown to-day behind the prison walls. I thank my precious Saviour that with my own two eyes I have witnessed this great love towards these outcasts of society. For it is Christ who is the only one who can put them back together and to mend them and turn them into precious vessels.

Yes, he is the answer. Though many will give up on them, Christ will always be there with that outstretched arm. Again it is the wondrous grace of God, which is being demonstrated to the inmate.

What a wonderful Saviour and Friend!

Chapter Twenty-three

～A Day to Remember ～

Earlier on, in a previous chapter, I spoke about an inmate called Dee, who was supernaturally healed by the power of God from a shoulder injury, which he had for six years. Dee worked in the education building and told me that one of the Prison Officers there was suffering with a bad back. He testified to this guy about God touching him.

So he explained to him that I would call over and pray for him. For a number of weeks I was calling in to see if he was in work. On the first two occasions he was off because of his back. The third week he was back at work. I called to see him. I briefly spoke to him a little bit about the Ministry. I then asked him if I could pray for him. He had explained to me that he had spent a lot of money to get the problem sorted out.

For twelve years he had had a curved spine. I prayed for him and then asked him how he felt. He got up out of his chair and started to move around. After a few minutes he asked me to check the way he was standing. Because of the curved spine he could not stand straight. He was always lop sided. So when he stood in front of me he looked completely normal. He commented that in twelve years he never stood so straight. We walked out into the corridor, he had then been completely straightened out by the power of God. He was completely dumb-struck and in awe.

From that moment he walked like a sergeant major, shoulders back and spine healed. This was amazing to witness. Again what a powerful testimony! He was going back to the chiropractor, to have his back checked and x-rayed. I would love to have been there to have seen the look on the chiropractor's face.

The following week I called to see the Prison Officer in the Education Building. We spoke about the miracle, which had taken place the previous week. He went on to tell me that when he was going home that day, he got into his car and had to adjust his mirror because now he was straight and upright. He visited the chiropractor during the week. He was amazed to see him standing so straight and said, "I see you have been working hard with those exercises". He had not been doing any exercises. He told me that when the chiropractor said this, the hairs on the back of his neck stood up. For he knew exactly that it was God who had touched him. When I sat with him he told me that he had no pain.

We both went to leave at the same time, on leaving he dropped his pen on the floor. Without any problem at all he bent over and picked up his pen from the floor. He said, "I could not have done this last week before you prayed with me". After twelve years all pain had gone. When he shared this with me he told me that at least 5 or 6 times a day he thinks about what took place the day God met with him and touched him. With tears in his eyes he would speak about the miracle he experienced. He also testified to the chiropractor what took place.

I asked him to write down all that took place that day, his testimony is as follows: -

For twelve years I have been suffering from lower back pain. Doctors have been unable to help with this problem, and more or less told me that I just had to live with it.

In mid June 2004 I went to a chiropractor who x-rayed my back and discovered that my spine was misaligned quite badly. He was confident that he could help, so I agreed to a course of treatment that would last for three months. The next x-ray was set for the end of July.

As a result of talking to a prisoner, Martin Tuson came to see me at the beginning of July. Martin introduced himself and explained how he knew of my back problem and how he felt that he could help.

As we prayed Martin asked God to cure my back problem. I have to admit I was a bit unsure of this actually happening.

Immediately after the prayer I felt different, I felt taller and felt straighter.

On the next visit to my chiropractor he could not understand how my posture was so good and wanted to do an x-ray of my spine. After the x-ray he told me that I must have been doing an awful lot of exercises because my spine was straight, and had not expected it to get to this stage until at least mid August.

I had not been doing any exercises.

This was a powerful miracle and I remember that day, feeling God's power strongly.

Only minutes after, I was guided by the Holy Spirit to visit an inmate who desperately needed to sense God's presence. He had been praying for God to draw closer to him. I called with him and he shared with me certain things for which he wanted prayer. We had a powerful time of prayer and afterwards he told me that he felt God's presence so strongly. This was a day that I would remember. I then went to call with David who had been lead to the Lord only a few weeks before. He had been moved to another part of the prison. He was doubled up. There was not a lot of room with a double bunk in a cell. When I walked into his cell he was sitting on the top bunk. The other young guy in with him was sitting on the only chair in the cell. He looked rather uncomfortable. David said, "Martin, I am going down hill. This guy has got me back on drugs. I am messing up big time". I told David not to worry, there was a reason that God had put him in with this other young guy.

I struck up a conversation with this young man. It turned out that five months before he had converted to the Muslim faith. I was interested to hear what made him choose this religion. "It seemed like the thing to do. I tried everything else", he said. He knew that David had just become a Christian and he was trying to break him. He had a copy of the Koran in his cell and every week he went to a special service with four other inmates.

I was amazed to find out that this young guy had previously accepted Christ into his heart in October 1999 whilst in prison. "What happened?" I asked him. He went on to explain that he had felt peace in his life when accepting Christ but when he was released, it was back out with the mates on drink and drugs and back in prison. We chatted and I told him of God's power within Maghaberry and other prisons. We spoke about many of the miracles that had taken place.

Then I realised why this young inmate was uncomfortable; he was hurting in great pain from a problem with his stomach. Apparently he was passing blood. When I was aware of this I asked him if I could pray and ask God to touch him and heal him. He was shocked. "Get away", he said, amazed that I would suggest such a thing. I told him that God loved him and that He would show his love towards him. He finally was happy that I prayed with him. I prayed and asked him how he was feeling. He bolted up out of his seat and started to shout and curse. "What's happened to me? I feel no more pain". "What did you do and how?". He started to sob and he made a lunge for me. He didn't know whether to hug me or shake my hand. He was healed instantly again by the power of God. This young fellow felt God's power in such a way that he was completely on a high. "Drugs have never made me feel like this", he said.

Again I told him God loved him so much that he healed him. "It's about time, my friend you give your life back to the Lord. Do you think Allah would have healed you?"

"I don't want anything to do with that anymore", he replied.

He wrote this testimony: -

Well I am 26 years old and I have been in and out of prison for the last 11 years, for all sorts of crimes, from car theft to armed robbery and I am doing 12 months now for A.B.H. When I was growing up I went to Sunday school and church. I always found it really enjoyable, but as I had started getting into trouble with the law I had stopped going to church. While I was in prison, I still got into trouble and I always seemed to end up in the punishment block and it was there that I smashed my cell up one night. When the stuff had been cleaned up, all that was left in my cell was me and a Bible, so I started reading it, and that night I gave myself to the Lord and asked him to change my life and help me (The date was 26th October 1999). As I had smashed my cell up, I had nothing in my cell. No toilet, no windows, nothing and I knew I would not get my cell fixed for up to a month, but the next day I went on a visit and when I came back to my cell it was fixed. (God had started to help me already). Well, I had finished my sentence with no more trouble, so I started going to church again. But after two months I stopped going and I started back on drugs and getting into trouble. I had turned my back on the Lord. While I was on remand I had started getting depressed a lot and started taking lots of drugs to black out a lot of things and I had been so angry that I became a Muslim but I was never really happy. Then I was doubled up with a guy called David, and about five days later I met Martin. I told Martin I had been with the Lord and we got talking and he asked me if I was in any pain as God could heal me. Martin prayed for the pain in my stomach to go away but to be honest I thought Martin was a bit mad. However I had this weird feeling and then there was no more pain. I could not believe it I jumped for joy and I felt like I was going to cry and I asked how he had done that. He said he did nothing (God did it). I thought, "Yes you are right." Now I know God is with me and loves me or He would not have done this and I will never forget that day or you, Martin. (Thanks) for opening my eyes again.

God Bless.
Ian

P.S. Will you pray for me, Martin? (Thank You)

I have tried my best to put this into words but it is difficult. You would have had to be in that cell to experience all that took place. It was incredible. As I left the prison that day, I sensed God's power so much that I had trouble walking in a straight line. A truly amazing day and out of all the two and a half years I have been going into Maghaberry, this was one of the most powerful days I have experienced. Praise God yet again for his love towards the inmate.

I could not wait to get back to visit Ian, who had been touched in a mighty way. The following week I called to see him. I found out that he had been moved the previous day to H.M.P Magilligan, (another prison in Northern Ireland). I spoke to his cellmate who witnessed the incredible miracle the previous week. He said to me, "Martin, the following day Ian gathered up all his Muslim bits and pieces including the Koran and left them to be thrown out". He then got a Bible. Praise God he returned to the Father.

Apparently Ian was telling other inmates about how he had been healed by the Lord. This is a powerful testimony and clearly shows the compassion of Christ towards the inmate even someone who once accepted him as Saviour. I believe Ian will carry this powerful testimony the rest of his life. It was a day that I certainly won't forget.

It is so wonderful to sense God's presence within the prison cell, for there is no wall thick enough to stop Christ's Grace, Mercy, Love and wonderful forgiveness from entering.

I remember hearing a powerful story about two Christian inmates who were making their way back to their cell, after Sunday morning service in the Chapel. As they walked, they came across an unusual sight. Up high on the prison wall they spotted a beautiful flower. It was growing from the wall. It looked so out of place they thought. Later on they found out that it was not a flower but a weed. God spoke to them through such an illustration. He told them that despite their condition he loved them so much and they were beautiful to him.

A powerful illustration.

When you think about it, where does man keep his most prized possessions? He keeps them under lock and key. There are many precious and prized inmates who are locked away, again this is a good definition of how God thinks towards the inmate.

I received a wonderful blessing through a letter, which arrived from a Brother in Christ serving a life sentence in Maghaberry.

Hi Martin,

Just thought I'd say, "Hello" and "Thank you"

Martin, God has done so much for me. His grace and blessing he has not kept from my presence in all of his blessings. I think of you, that through this sentence which I fully deserve, in his compassion, he has sent you, a reflection of his character, that the time you give to me, you share in my sentence. Unjustly you do time with every prisoner in here who God sends you to.

Thank you for giving up time which you could spend with your family or friends to spend with us. In our prayers you are remembered 2 Thess 1:3-5

May God continue to work through you and may the spirit continue to give you strength and oil, as you shine the light of faith while walking through these darkened cells.

I pray that His blessings are endless on you and your family and the fruits of the spirit pour throughout.

Thanks again for everything if ever anything could ever be done to repay your kindness or show our appreciation, please don't hesitate to ask.

Yours in Christ
Scottie

God's timing is perfect and as I always say, there are no coincidences with Him. Many times, as I walk the wings, I am lead by the Spirit of God to certain inmates. On one of these occasions I was lead to the punishment unit to visit one of the young guys. God had been challenging this young man and speaking to him. When I met with him he told me that he believed that God was speaking to him. He could not get this out of his mind. He had asked to see a chaplain. No one came and he started to get frustrated. Then that very same day he received a letter and book that I had sent. This encouraged him.

As we talked I sensed that the Lord had most definitely brought me along at the correct time. I explained to him about Christ and the cross and the way of Salvation.

Praise God he received Christ as his personal Saviour that day. Yes, he still struggles with certain things but God is working in his life and using him in the prison.

On another occasion, again God's appointment I spoke with another young 22-year-old lad. He was struggling with prison life and had tried to end his life many times. I shared my testimony with him and shared some scriptures from the word of God. He told me that on many occasions he had tried to ask God into his life. It turned out that he would always try to get himself sorted out and cleaned up, so that he would be fit to be accepted by Christ. I told him that we would always be trying to strive and be our best. "Come as you are," I told him. "He will take you and accept you now, no matter your past, you can be forgiven this very day". He wanted so much to be accepted by Christ and to know that he would have a home in Heaven. I lead him in a prayer of Salvation, he mumbled and struggled with his words, but Praise God he knew that he was sincere and he meant every word from his heart. When we had finished praying, there was a silence. I looked at him and then he gave me the broadest smile. I could see nearly everyone of his teeth.

"I feel a bit different", he said.

"God has come into your life," I said. We spoke about prayer and Bible reading. I said to him that today was the start of a new life for him. The old had gone, he was now a child of the living God. There is no real way to describe the feelings that I experience within the prison cell when I witness these young inmates accepting Christ into their lives.

Again the power of God unto Salvation.

Chapter Twenty-four

∼ Broken Chains ∼

No matter whether it is through letter writing, the telephone, or personal contact with the inmate, God is moving in an amazing way. Chains are indeed being broken and the captives are being set free.

Isaiah 61: V 1 says "The spirit of the Lord God is upon me: because the Lord hath anointed me to preach good tidings unto the meek: he hath sent me to bind up the broken hearted, to proclaim liberty to the captives, and the opening of the prison to them that are bound."

Throughout this world at this present moment of time there is a mighty move of God's Holy Spirit within many prisons. God is doing a new thing in these last days. Yes, these incarcerated men and women are in prison for a reason. They have committed crimes and they have to be punished. But Praise God, for his wondrous Grace, mercy, love and forgiveness, towards these outcasts of society. I have sat with many inmates over these past few years and physically witnessed the love that Christ has for them. Words can't fully describe what I have and am indeed witnessing.

One inmate once stopped me and asked me what I was doing in the prison. I explained to him that I was a Christian, bringing the good news of the Gospel to the inmates.

I will never forget what he said to me. "You know something. God is not interested in criminals and thugs like me". How wrong he was. It opened up an excellent opportunity for me to tell him about Christ. The fact that it was the so-called "Outcasts of Society" that he spent most of his time with. This young guy never knew this. To think that God is only interested in good people. What a lie from the devil!

As I said, a price has to be paid for the crimes that have been committed. But God, if he wanted to could intervene at anytime and have anyone of his children released. I write to many on death row in different countries. I do not believe in the death penalty. Many Christian inmates do not want to be released because they want to stay and reach out to their fellow inmates.

That is commitment. The fact remains that Christ has a plan and purpose for everyone of their lives. Each one of God's children who are behind bars could write their own book on how God has sustained them during their sentence, for example, Scotties letter in a previous chapter. At the end of the day, as I tell Brothers and Sisters in prison, it does not matter what people in the world say about them. It's what God says that matters. For they will stand before Christ one day, not man. God is raising up men and women who have served time in prison and today they are pastoring churches and being used to evangelize through out the world. This following scripture sums this up.

Corinthians 1:27-28
"But God hath chosen the foolish things of the world to confound the wise; and God hath chosen the weak things of the world to confound the things which are mighty. And base things of the world, and things which are despised, hath God chosen, yes, and things which are not, to bring to nought things that are."

As you have seen in the pages of this book God is moving within the darkness of the prison cell. I have shared only a small amount of what has taken place in my life over the last four years. This book should be an encouragement to those who read it. I know that God will speak to many through it.

At times I can relate to how Moses felt when he was asked to go to Pharaoh and ask for the children of Israel to be released from their bondage and later when Moses came to the Red Sea. This has been like my own Red Sea experience. Seeing God move in and through my life in a most incredible way.

Again as I stated at the beginning of this book, all of the Glory and praise go to my Lord and Saviour Jesus Christ. What the future holds remains to be seen.

All I know is that God will continue to use me to reach out his love and grace towards those afflicted and needy men and women within the prison walls. Through the passage of scripture in Habakkuk 1:5 God has spoken to me. This verse says that "he will work a work that I will not even believe with my own eyes." Praise his Holy name forever!

Chapter Twenty-five

∼ An Inmates Perspective ∼

For the last Chapter of this book I have asked a precious Brother and friend in Christ to write an inmate's perspective. How God is moving in Maghaberry Prison amongst inmates. You will hear from him what he has experienced over these last few years.

Thank you

Dear Friend,
Peace and love to you in the precious name of our Lord Jesus Christ. I have been incarcerated for the last ten years, a sentence that I rightly deserve. Three years ago God convicted me through the Holy Sprit and poured His Grace over me.

Over two thousand years ago our Lord visited the earth. He sat amongst sinners curing the lame and healing the sick. Why should today be any different? From inside the prison walls, our risen King still continues with the same love and compassion. I have been blessed and privileged to be a witness of the miracles, which I now write and testify to you.

Two years ago during a football match, I received an injury to my left leg. This resulted in damaged ligaments and my needing keyhole surgery. Limping about the landing one day a Christian by the name of Martin Tuson asked me if he could pray for my leg. I was rather sceptical about healing and miracles. Don't get me wrong being a new creation is one thing, yet to see God's power flow through another being is another! So I told him to go ahead. He prayed and asked me if I felt any different. Well, to be honest with you, I tried to put all my weight on my leg and it took the pressure. Yet I still had discomfort. I thanked him for his prayer, although I could not stop thinking that I probably could have done that without his prayer. It's funny. Having been given the gift of faith from God I still found it easier to exercise doubt!

I have watched Martin pray for an inmate who got his finger severed in a mixing accident. The prisoner got the digit knitted to the bone and was told by the doctor that he would be lucky if he would have movement again. Every Friday Martin would leave his cell and still no joy. You could see I was starting to think this guy should be in the cell next to me.

Then one day my friend hurt his back lifting a flowerpot, of all things. Watching him in agony as he gripped the frame of his bed, as spasms which seemed to indicate a slipped disc. He twisted and contorted in pain. Martin came along and he asked my friend, "Do you mind if I prayed for you?" I think he would have said 'yes' to brain surgery, he would have tried anything that might help. Again Martin prayed and this time I saw the look of fear and bewilderment on my friend's face. He got up out of bed, feeling no pain. He touched his toes and laughed. Another inmate entered his cell and he just started wrestling with him. The prisoner gave his life to God. When you have shared in that experience, you can only fall on your knees and Praise God.

God's Spirit has healed many prisoners through Martin's ministry from heart problems, shoulder pains, stomach problems, and others that I have heard of. The "Set Free" ministry and magazines testify to these. It has spread the communication of the love of God through prisons across the world and led many to following Christ.

Like myself at the start, I believe many who read this would doubt of these miracles. I am not writing to prove God's power. His creation and son do that for me. I just want to share in the hope that some may rejoice and be strengthened in knowing that Jesus has not forsaken us or left us, just as he promised.

You may ask yourself, "Why prison?"

Why should God's love be demonstrated amongst people who cause others pain?

I can only reply to that by saying, "It is the sick that need a physician, not the righteous."

Maybe by God demonstrating his power and love inside these prison walls is a witness to us sinners of the love that we need to give back

What else could change a man's life, but God? James, 5: 15-16.

No words could ever thank Martin, for giving up time outside with your family and friends to visit us in jail. Through your love and help you have been a true reflection of Christ. On behalf of the prisoners that you have witnessed to and whose lives you have touched, we give thanks. In prayer to our father, we ask that He continue to bless you and your family. We pray that your kindness through Christ is repaid back in heavenly rewards and that He bestows on your head a crown that will make our king proud, Isaiah. 58:8

Your Friend and faithful servants in Christ.

My prayer is that God will bless you and that you will come to know the power of God in your own life. When you next hear the word 'prison' mentioned either on the news or in the newspaper, remember what you have just read.

Philippians 1:6 "Being confident of this very thing that he which hath begun a good work in you will perform it until the day of Jesus Christ."

All scriptures are taken from the King James Version of the Bible.

Acknowledgements

I would like to thank the following people, Pastor David Beckett for writing the Foreword. Thanks also to all of my Brothers and Sisters in the Ministry especially to Eileen Reeves (Palm Tree Ministry), and John Wilson. I would also like to thank all of the inmates who wrote their testimonies. For my Brothers in the Lord in H.M.P. Maghaberry, especially Scottie for the inspiring title of this book. To my family, Margaret my wife for all the support and help with this Ministry. There are no words to thank her for being there through the ups and downs and for her putting up with me, especially when my time has been taken up with the Lords work. My Mother and Father again for their encouragement with this book. A big thanks to Robert and Liz Stewart, especially to Liz for the preparation and many long hours spent in the making of this book. Thanks also to the other members of this Ministry Eric, Mark and Christine for their dedication.

To Brother Dougie March, for all of his prayers and support.

Most of all I want to give my Heavenly Father all of the Glory and Praise for every page in this book.

Contact: -

Martin Tuson
Set Free Prison Ministries Bangor
75 Towerview Avenue
Bangor
Co. Down
N. Ireland
BT19 6BT

Bangor

Website: www.setfreeprisonministriesbangor.com

Printed in the United Kingdom
by Lightning Source UK Ltd.
109303UKS00001B/178-288